Small Miracles
for the
Jewish Heart

Extraordinary Coincidences from

Yesterday and Today

Yitta Halberstam
&
Judith Leventhal

D0190139

ADAMS MEDIA CORPORATION
Avon, Massachusetts

In loving memory of Rabbi Shlomo Carlebach:
He had the greatest Jewish heart of all.
— Yitta Halberstam and Judith Leventhal

Published by Adams Media Corporation
57 Littlefield Street, Avon, MA 02322
Visit the Adams Media home page at *www.adamsmedia.com* and
the *Small Miracles* home page at *www.adamsmedia.com/smallmiracles.*

ISBN: 1-58062-548-7

Printed in Canada.

J I H G F E D C B A

Library of Congress Cataloging-in-Publication Data
available from the publisher.

Cover illustration by Michael Muchnik.

This book is available at quantity discounts for bulk purchases.
For information, call 1-800-872-5627.

Permissions
Grateful acknowledgment is made to the following for permission to reprint
previously published material:
Jason Aronson Publishers, Northvale, N.J. for a selection from "Holy
Brother: Inspiring Stories and Enchanted Tales About Rabbi Shlomo
Carlebach" by Yitta Halberstam Mandelbaum ©1997.
Prima Publishing, a division of Random House, for a story from "How We
Met" by Miriam Sokal ©1999.
Aish Hatorah Shabbat Shalom Weekly, for a story by Rabbi Kalman
Packousz. Free subscription available at *www.shabbatshalom.org.*
Art Scroll/Mesorah Publishers (*www.artscroll.com*) for a selection from
"The Maggid Speaks" by Rabbi Paysach Krohn.

Acknowledgments

Our thanks and appreciation go to: Rabbi Meir Fund, spiritual leader of the Flatbush Minyan, whose wisdom, guidance, inspiration, and input continues to be steadfast and strong; Aaron Breitbart of the Simon Wiesenthal Center for valuable help in tracking down and piecing together one of the stories in this book; Rabbi Kenneth Auman for so generously sharing the Nathan Straus story, and Barry Fleischmann for his exceptionally good-natured way in hunting for and delivering great stories.

Virginia Rubens, copyeditor extraordinaire, for making our prose sing; Leah Bloom and Kate Epstein, assistant editors, for their warm and gracious assistance in all matters; Pam Liflander for being one of the best editors any writer could ever hope for in her lifetime; and Gary Krebs, Editorial Director of Adams Media, for picking up the pieces so masterfully and doing such a fabulous job.

Sarah Piel, Katharine Drayton, Lorie Entenman, and Richard Pine of the Arthur Pine Agency for superb and wholehearted support of every kind; you guys are the tops!

Our friends who are blessings in our lives; our mothers, siblings, and in-laws who give us so much encouragement and support, and Anna Ashton, who makes it all possible, and has given us more than we ever could repay.

Special appreciation goes to the wonderful folks at Harnick's Bookstore — Noreen, Rose, Minnie, and Evan, and the Steg siblings — Yitzhak, Shloime, Chaim, Motty,

Sruli, and Feige—whose positive feedback and excitement about *Small Miracles* nurtures us always.

Gratitude also to Irene Klass of *The Jewish Press* for early childhood mentoring that made a tremendous impact, and her daughter Naomi Mauer, who walks in her parents' footsteps and continues to perpetuate a great legacy.

Our treasures, our joys, our ports-in-the-storm, and havens: our husbands and children. Motty, Jules, Yossi, Eli, Arielle, and Shira: you are the miracles in our lives, and we thank God every day for such magnificent and abundant gifts.

This book is dedicated to the loving memory of Rabbi Shlomo Carlebach, known throughout the world as "The Singing Rabbi" or "The Hippie Rabbi." For more than four decades, this inspired personality reached out to Jews of all persuasions, offering them succor, solace, and sanctuary. He gave of himself ceaselessly, unstintingly, tirelessly, and he illuminated the darkness for hundreds of thousands.

We miss you Shlomo, and the void is deep without you. We tell your stories and sing your songs and try to follow your example as best as we can. But no one has your heart, Shlomo, the one heart that sang with such unconditional love and infectious joy, the heart that miraculously expanded to embrace an entire universe.

With this book, we pay tribute to and remember with great affection a Jewish heart that was as wide as the world it encompassed.

— *Yitta Halberstam and Judith Leventhal*

Introduction

It is a hot, dry, windless day. The atmosphere is so stagnant, that the very air shimmers with intense heat. No branches sway, no leaf stirs—all is motionless and still. Against this torpid backdrop, a man—in sharp relief to the indolence of the day—is seen rushing down the street. Intent on his own personal mission, he does not notice the leaden sluggishness that surrounds him. He is immersed in his own thoughts, and the conspicuous lack of a breeze, the absence of currents rippling through the blades of grass near him, barely intrude upon his consciousness.

Suddenly, on this very day when nothing else moves, a single leaf plummets to the ground. The man pauses for a fraction of a second, but does not stop to wonder *why* or *how*. After all, this is a commonplace, ordinary event that he has just observed, is it not? Leaves glide and drift and float off trees every day, don't they? Nothing consequential has occurred. Just a haphazard, normal act of nature that occurs all the time. The man shrugs his shoulders in indifference and marches on. He does not know that what he has just witnessed is a miracle.

For on the sidewalk beneath the man's feet, a little worm, unseen by the naked human eye, has just cried out to God: "God, it is *so* hot today! I am broiling under the blazing sun! Can't you please send me a little shade?" And God, who has infinite mercy on all his creatures, even tiny worms, responds immediately to the heartfelt plea. But the man, whose vision is limited, whose comprehension is circumscribed, is oblivious to the small drama that has just taken place. He only sees the plummeting leaf; he does not see the worm on the ground. The man is completely unaware of the fact that he has just watched an act of God.

"We do not see things as *they* are," the Talmud tells us, "we see things as *we* are." We human beings filter reality through the prism of our already entrenched beliefs, prejudices, and biases. Our perceptual abilities are enormously affected and influenced by our subjective feelings. Even when we think we are seeing reality clearly, we may not be seeing it at all.

A famous scientist once reported a fascinating phenomenon: He had traveled to the (then) remote island of Micronesia, whose primitive natives had no conception of the realities of the modern world to which we are so inured. The natives were terrified by the electronic products the scientist showed them, convinced that it was some magical power that made them work. But what truly startled the scientist and his team of researchers was the insight they gleaned about the power of preconceived notions and man's inability to see that which he can't understand. When a platoon of ships sailed near the island of Micronesia and came into view, the scientists excitedly pointed them out to the natives. And then a puzzling, bizarre, unfathomable thing occurred. Although the ships were clearly visible to the scientists, the natives—who had never seen a ship before—could not see them at all. *They did not see the ships because they could not comprehend them.* They were outside the milieu of their experience and thus beyond their perception.

The two stories above, must, by necessity, make us feel humble and small shaking our certainties and confidence. How much of life's mysteries are we really seeing—and grasping? What about its miracles? When we say "Well, nothing miraculous ever happens to *me,*" are we perhaps making this statement from a place of unawareness—or ingratitude? Could it be that life is actually permeated with small miracles every day, but we just don't see them? We are finite beings after all; how can we even presume to penetrate the Finite Mind?

"That which the caterpillar calls the end of life, the master calls a butterfly," the novelist Richard Bach has said. Could it be that the ordinary events of day-to-day life are in fact not picayune happenstance, but small miracles instead? How differently we would experience life, if we would live with eyes filled with wonder, considering each day through the prism of "radical amazement" as a theologian once described it.

The history of the Jewish people is drenched in miracles: apocalyptic, sublime, grandiose, and breathtaking. Sadly, in contemporary times, we are not privileged to witness the scope and grandeur of God's miracles in the same manner as our forefathers did, but we do experience the "coincidences" that attest to God's presence. These are gentle taps on our shoulder to remind us that God is with us always, even in the ordinary details of day-to-day life.

We hope that with this fifth book of *Small Miracles* we will be able to help nudge you awake. To the awe, the mystery, the wonder of a Higher Power orchestrating our lives with infinite care and attention—through the medium that some mistakenly call "coincidences," but that we firmly know to be nothing less than miracles.

May we all be blessed with the wakefulness and wisdom to know them when they come into our lives. We are fuller and better people when we recognize and acknowledge God's hand; we vibrate with joy and gratitude—for God, for the universe, and for all its creatures with whom we are interconnected in a great field of spiritual energy laden with meaning, order, and love.

"*H*ello, Mr. Klein?" The voice of Goldie Buxbaum,* budding matchmaker, bubbled over with excitement.

It was difficult enough to find the right soul mates for the young in the Orthodox Jewish community, but it was truly a Herculean feat to make a match for the above-thirty set. This was the population over which tearful mothers sighed, sobbed, and wrung their hands in utter despair while their more successful counterparts (*grandmothers* already!) groaned in commiseration and offered to call their friend in *Australia,* who might . . . possibly . . . know someone who was available and under *seventy.*

Because there was such a dearth of eligible young men for women over thirty, Goldie Buxbaum felt downright jubilant as she dialed the telephone number of Joseph Klein, a wonderful but still unattached male of thirty-five. She had just met a young woman of thirty-one who seemed to fulfill all the criteria on his wish list, and Goldie was firmly convinced that this was the woman for Mr. Klein. Goldie was, in fact, so excited about the match that she barely waited for Mr. Klein's return greeting before she plunged headlong into the purpose of her call.

*Note: Names followed by an asterisk are pseudonyms.

"Listen," she practically shrieked in excitement, "I have found your soul mate, your destined one. The most wonderful woman in the whole world. And she's just the right age for you . . . thirty-one!"

As Goldie paused to collect her breath, Mr. Klein interrupted her with an apologetic cough and a dry inquiry.

"Thirty-one?" he said in a puzzled voice. "Don't you think," he protested politely, "that she's just a little bit too young for me?"

For once in her life, Goldie was at a loss for words. She was stunned. What was the matter with the man? Of all the strange excuses! Maybe he wasn't really sincere about getting married, after all? All the men she had dealt with in the past had insisted on much younger women as potential mates, and now Mr. Klein found a four-year difference to be *too* much?

"Are you crazy?" Goldie screeched. "What's wrong with a four-year difference?"

"What are you talking about . . . a four-year difference?" he sputtered on the other end. "I'm sixty-five!"

"Sixty-five?" Goldie squawked, comprehension finally starting to dawn. "Wait a second . . . who *is* this? I thought you said you're Mr. Klein."

"Yes . . . I certainly *am* Mr. Klein. But who, may I ask, are *you*?"

"One minute, one minute," Goldie labored, her mind racing. "Is this Mr. *Joseph* Klein?"

"This is Mr. Klein, but my first name is *Tibor*."

There was a pause. Then an exclamation: "I must have the *wrong* number!"

"Well . . . this is pretty funny," the stranger on the other end laughed. "And to think I was actually getting my hopes up about a possible match!"

Goldie's ears perked up. Always one to seize an opportunity, she did not stammer an apology and hang up. Instead, like radar honing in on its target, her antennae shot up to an all-new vertical high.

"You are *single*?" She pounced on Mr. Klein.

"I'm widowed," he said, "and actually I am looking to remarry. Are you a matchmaker? You wouldn't by any chance have someone closer to my age, would you?"

"Well . . . I'm sure I can come up with someone, although I can't think of anyone in particular right now . . ." she said distractedly. Her attention was diverted by a constant beeping on her line, indicating that another call was coming in. She hated call waiting! She had ignored the beeps during the entire conversation, but the caller on the other line was persistent, and the beeps were stretching her nerves taut. *Maybe something was wrong with one of the kids in school? Maybe it was an emergency?* She really should answer the beep.

"Listen, Mr. Klein, can you hold on for a minute? I have to answer my call waiting. I'll be right back."

I hope I don't disconnect him, she thought anxiously, as she pressed the "flash" button and clicked onto the next call. *This better be important.*

"Goldie, dear, I'm so sorry to bother you, but I was wondering when your mother-in-law will be arriving in New York next week." It was her mother-in-law's old friend, Sarah Rubin.* Sarah and Goldie's mother-in-law, Faige, kept in touch intermittently. The last time she had spoken to Sarah had been about six months earlier, and she would never even have thought to remember the sweet-tempered widow if her call hadn't come in at such an auspicious time.

Light bulbs flashed, alarm bells rang, and neon signs blinked furiously in Goldie Buxbaum's fertile brain.

"Sarah!" she said impulsively. "Are you seeing anyone right now?"

"No, unfortunately I'm not," Sarah said wistfully. "Why do you ask?"

"Sarah, can you hold on for a minute?" Goldie said without responding to her question. "I have someone on the other line . . ." She clicked back to Mr. Klein and announced with a surge of triumph in her voice, "Mr. Klein, have I got a match for you!"

Five years later, Tibor Klein and Sarah Rubin are happily married and living in Borough Park, Brooklyn.

"I was originally upset when I realized I had gotten a wrong number," reflects Goldie. "But in retrospect, it wasn't the *wrong* number at all. God made me push all the right buttons!"

Even before war clouds thickened over eastern Europe in the pre-Nazi years, it became common for Jews in the besieged countries—tired of pogroms, poverty, and despair—to send their children to the United States, where opportunities for a better life beckoned.

From the early 1900s on, parents scrimped and saved their rubles to pay for the long and arduous voyage of their sons and daughters, who traveled alone aboard unseaworthy vessels that offered inhuman conditions and an uncertain fate. Since tickets for each treacherous journey cost a small fortune and exacted a heavy toll on the destitute families, parents often chose to ship their children to America one by one rather than sending them all at once. But it was always their hope and dream that all the children would eventually reach the American haven, where they would be joined later by their parents. In the interim, they would stay with relatives who would care for them and help them wait, sometimes for months or years. And sometimes the longed-for reunions never took place at all.

Anya Gold* was the chosen one in her family. She was the eldest of eight, and in 1930 her Polish parents told her it was time to go. They had saved just enough money for one ticket, and had decided that Anya would be the first child to leave. They would all soon join her, they said.

Growing up in Baltimore under the sheltering wing of an affectionate aunt, Anya waited for her family to arrive. But they never did.

It took years for the family to accumulate enough money for another fare, and by then they had been caught in Hitler's web. In Baltimore, over the years, Anya had received the occasional letter from Poland recounting family news and milestones—her siblings' bar mitzvahs, their marriages, the births of grandchildren. She awaited these letters eagerly and savored each one. And then the letters came no more.

Anya feared the worst, but it was only after the war that she was able to conclusively determine her family's fate. A few stray survivors from her hometown in Poland who trickled into Baltimore in the late 1940s brought the news she had both known and dreaded to hear: Her entire family had been wiped out. They had all perished in the camps.

It was hard to go on afterwards, but even the survivors began to rebuild their lives. Her family's memory burned in her mind, heart, and soul, but Anya knew that the best way for her to commemorate their legacy was by creating one herself. She would marry and have many children, she vowed. And each would carry one of her siblings' names.

Anya did indeed marry a wonderful man named Sol, and their life together was almost idyllic. They were truly soul mates, and their love ran deep. They longed for children—flesh of their flesh, blood of their blood—but in this one area, they were thwarted. It was the only thorn in their otherwise perfect union. They were childless.

After many years of trying, of seeking help from specialists the world over, Anya and Sol confronted the reality of their situation. "Would you want to adopt?" Anya asked Sol one day in a tentative voice.

Anya had considered this option for a long time, but inwardly she had rebelled. She didn't want to raise someone else's children. She wanted to cradle her own newborn in her arms. She couldn't imagine that she would feel the same way about an adopted child. Still, there seemed no other recourse. They were never going to have children of their own, the doctors had pronounced—a death knell to their hopes and dreams.

Her husband was more certain. "Yes, let's adopt," he urged.

They contacted a Jewish agency in New York and were told that an infant had just been given up for adoption by its teenage mother. They traveled to New York with growing excitement, but when they arrived their hopes were dashed. The flustered agency official stammered an apology. "I'm so sorry," she said, "but the grandmother has decided to raise the baby, after all."

Had their trip to New York been a total waste?

"You know," the agency official remarked, "I do have

a wonderful little girl named Miriam who is in desperate need of a home."

Miriam was adorable and endearing, but she was already eight years old. Although Anya and Sol reluctantly agreed to meet the child, and were captivated by her sweet appeal, they couldn't quite come to terms with her age. "I really wanted a child young enough to know me as its only mother," Anya explained. "I want a newborn to cradle in my arms."

"I understand," the agency official said. "But Miriam has really been through a lot in her short lifetime, and could really use a loving home."

"Sorry, but no," Anya said, with regret.

A year passed with no prospects. Anya had contacted many agencies across the United States, but an infant was increasingly difficult to find. All the while, Anya's intense longing for a child consumed her being—a hungry and hollow ache.

"You know," she mused to her husband one day, "maybe we were too quick to dismiss adopting Miriam. She was really an exceptionally appealing child. Something about her actually tugged at my heartstrings in a special way."

Sol looked at her thoughtfully. "It's been a full year," he said. "Do you think she's still available?"

She was, the agency official told them over the phone.

"Not too many people want a nine-year-old," she explained mournfully, "So, yes, she's still available. . . .

But there's a complication," she added. "Her little brother's been found in Europe and has joined her in our Home for War Orphans. The siblings are inseparable, and we've promised them that they'll be adopted together. Would you consider two?"

Back in New York, Anya and Sol met the siblings and once again, Anya felt drawn to Miriam's sweet demeanor. Her six-year-old brother Moishe was adorable, too.

Anya and Sol looked at each other silently, telegraphing their mental agreement. *Let's do it!* their eyes said.

Back in Baltimore, Anya shepherded the two children across the threshold into their new home, and they glanced at the furnishings with eyes of wonder. Little Moishe was shy and restrained, but Miriam was adventurous and curious, and she moved around the living room excitedly, touching the knickknacks and curios that adorned the mantels and tables. Suddenly, she stopped short in front of the piano and her face went white. She pointed to a photograph. In a tight and strained voice, Miriam asked, "Why do you have a picture of my *bubbe* (grandmother) on your piano?"

"What?" Anya asked, confused.

"My *bubbe*. Why is my *bubbe's* picture on your piano?"

Anya stared at the portrait of her deceased mother. What in heaven's name was the little girl talking about?

Miriam ran to the lone piece of luggage she had

brought with her from the orphanage. From a battered pouch, she retrieved a faded photo and brought it to Anya's side. "See," she said, pointing. "I have the same picture, too. My *bubbe*."

"My mother," Anya whispered almost inaudibly.

"Do you want to see a picture of my mommy?" Miriam asked. She raced to the luggage to retrieve another photograph. "Do you want to see what she looked like?" She handed Anya a picture of someone she knew very well.

"*Sarah!*" Anya screamed, as her knees buckled beneath her.

"How do you know my mother's name?" the child asked in confusion.

Unknowingly, Anya had adopted the two orphaned children of her dead sister, Sarah.

They were flesh of her flesh, blood of her blood.

They were . . . her own.

*S*am Lowinger* missed his rendezvous with death not once, but twice, on the morning of September 11th. A successful businessman with offices in the World Trade Center, he was scheduled to depart New York on Tuesday, September 11th for a meeting on the West Coast. On Monday afternoon, for no apparent reason, he suddenly decided to postpone his flight. He called his travel agent and asked if he could take an evening flight instead. The travel agent said that there were seats available on other planes leaving later that day and that he could easily make the scheduling change. A new flight was subsequently booked.

Now that the morning of September 11th was suddenly freed up, Sam decided to go ahead and schedule a breakfast meeting at his offices in the World Trade Center instead. He called the meeting for nine o'clock in the morning.

Usually a punctual fellow, Sam tried to leave his home in Monsey, New York, early enough, but a variety of obstacles kept detaining him. On the road, he found himself further stonewalled by unusually heavy traffic. At nine o'clock in the morning, he was still en route to work when he heard the news of the terrorist attack on the radio. Shaken badly, Sam turned back home.

Later that day, his travel agent called him. "I'm in awe of how much God has blessed you," the agent said.

"I just feel horrendous about all those innocent people who died," Sam replied in a subdued voice, "so many of whom I personally know. But yes, of course, I am deeply grateful to God that I was late for the meeting."

"Late for the meeting?" the travel agent echoed back. "What meeting?"

"Isn't that what you meant when you said that God blessed me? I was supposed to be at the World Trade Center for a breakfast meeting at 9:00 A.M."

"You were also *supposed* to be on the flight from Newark to San Francisco that the terrorists rammed into the North Tower," the travel agent said. "That's the miracle I was talking about. You were scheduled to be on that hijacked flight this morning, and you suddenly canceled it yesterday, remember?"

"I didn't even know you had a 9:00 A.M. meeting at the World Trade Center this morning," the travel agent continued. "Oh my goodness!" she shrieked. "Do you realize what this means? You eluded death *twice* in one day. You had a double miracle!"

At the turn of the twentieth century, two of the wealthiest and most famous men in America were a pair of Jewish brothers named Nathan and Isidor Straus. Owners of R. H. Macy's Department Store and founders of the A&S (Abraham & Straus) chain, the brothers were multimillionaires, renowned for their philanthropy and social activism.

They vigorously supported a host of political and social causes and were considered to be among the leading economic thinkers of their time. Wielding great influence in many different orbits, they both occupied distinguished positions in local and national politics.

A warm friend of President Grover Cleveland, Isidor Straus was offered a position in his cabinet as postmaster general, but he declined, choosing instead to serve in Congress during the waning years of the nineteenth century. Nathan Straus served as parks commissioner of New York City and was responsible for organizing the campaign for compulsory pasteurization of milk. Both men commanded tremendous respect and awe from their colleagues and friends.

In 1912, the brothers and their wives were touring Europe, enjoying all the cultural riches of the Continent—the museums, the operas, the theaters, and the palaces—when Nathan, the more ardent Zionist of the two, impulsively said one day, "Hey, why don't we hop over to Palestine?"

Israel wasn't the tourist mecca then that it is today. Its population was ravaged by disease, famine, and poverty; but the two had a strong sense of solidarity with their less fortunate brethren, and they also wanted to see the health and welfare centers they had endowed with their millions. However, after a week spent touring the holy places, the fledgling cities, the yeshivas, and the artists' colonies, Isidor Straus had had enough. "How many camels, hovels, and yeshivas can you see?" he complained to Nathan, who was still endlessly enthralled by the country. "If you've seen one, you've seen them all. It's time to go," Isidor decreed with edgy impatience in his voice.

But Nathan refused to heed his brother's imperious command. It wasn't that he was oblivious to the hardships around him; it was precisely because of them that he wanted to stay. As he absorbed firsthand the vastness of the challenges his fellow Jews were coping with, he felt the burden of responsibility.

"We can't leave now," he protested. "Look how much work has to be done here. We have to help. We have the means to help. We can't turn our backs on our people."

"So we'll send more money," his brother snapped back. "I just want to get out of here."

But Nathan felt that money simply wasn't enough. He felt that the Jews who lived under such dire circumstances in Palestine needed the brothers' very presence among them: their initiative, their leadership, and their ideas. Isidor disagreed.

The two argued back and forth, and finally Isidor said, "If you insist, stay here. Ida and I are going back to America . . . where we belong."

The two separated. Isidor and his wife returned to Europe, while Nathan and his spouse stayed in Palestine, traveling the country and contributing huge sums of money to the establishment of educational, health, and social welfare programs to benefit the needy. Nathan also financed the creation of a brand-new city on the shores of the Mediterranean. And since his name in Hebrew was Natan, and he was the city's chief donor, the founders named it after him and called it . . . Natanya.

Meanwhile, back in Europe, Isidor Straus was preparing to sail home to America aboard an ocean liner for which he had also made reservations for his brother, Nathan, and his wife. "You must leave Palestine NOW!" he cabled his brother in an urgent telegram. "I have made reservations for you and if you don't get here soon, you'll miss the boat."

But Nathan delayed. There was so much work to be done that he waited until the last possible moment to make the connection. By the time he reached London, it was April 12 and the liner had already left port in Southampton with Isidor and Ida Straus aboard.

Nathan felt disconsolate that he had, as his brother had warned, "missed the boat." For this was no ordinary expedition, no common, everyday cruise that he had forfeited, but the much-ballyhooed maiden voyage of the most famous ship of the century.

Five days later, Isidor and Ida Straus were among the 1,500 passengers who perished in the tragic wreck of the *Titanic*. Heroically refusing to take advantage of the rule "Women and children first" and take her place in the lifeboats, Mrs. Straus insisted on staying on board with her husband of forty years. In turn, Isidor Straus was urged by crewmen to take a place in the lifeboat alongside his wife, but he would not do so as long as other women remained on board. The aged couple went down with the ship, together until the very end.

Meanwhile, Nathan Straus, grief-stricken and deeply mourning his brother and sister-in-law, could not shake off his sense that he had had a rendezvous with history. The knowledge that he had avoided death permeated his consciousness for the rest of this life, and until his death in 1931, he pursued his philanthropic activities with an intensity that was unrivaled in his time.

Today, Natanya is a scenic resort city of 200,000 and headquarters to Israel's thriving diamond trade — one of the most important industries in the country.

And in almost every part of the city, there is some small reminder of Nathan Straus's largesse, his humanity, and love for his people.

His legacy lives on.

A *certain* Israeli rabbi had a heart condition and was under a New York doctor's care. The rabbi always carried the doctor's phone number with him in case of emergency.

On one of the rabbi's trips to New York, he felt sharp chest pains and realized that he needed medical attention at once. He dialed the number and prayed that it wouldn't be busy. It rang twice and then a woman answered. The rabbi asked if the doctor was there.

"Yes," the woman said in surprise. "The doctor happens to be here."

When the doctor got to the phone he heard the symptoms and assured the rabbi that he would be there in a few moments.

"But how did you know that I was here?" asked the doctor. "I didn't tell anyone where I was going."

Now it was the rabbi's turn to be surprised.

"You're not in your office?" he asked in puzzlement.

"No, I'm on an emergency call a few blocks from my home," the doctor answered.

"But I just dialed your regular number," the incredulous rabbi insisted.

Then the doctor looked down at the phone from which he was speaking. The numbers were precisely the same as his office phone except for one, in which the number was one digit off! By inadvertently dialing one of the numbers incorrectly, the rabbi had actually dialed the "right" number!

Later, after having been taken to the hospital, the rabbi was told that his life had been saved only because he had reached the doctor in time.

Wrong number. Right party.

— *Rabbi Paysach Krohn*

*T*he nightmare was over, the rebuilding had begun.

At the end of World War II, Simon Wiesenthal was a young man grown old. He had survived the death camps, though barely, and was slowly healing in a DP (Displaced Persons) camp in Germany. Although his youth was behind him, his life lay before him, and his destiny was yet to be shaped.

In the concentration camps, he had surreptitiously drawn pictures of the atrocities even as they happened; committed to memory the brutal faces and names of the tormentors; emblazoned in his mind their heinous crimes and nefarious deeds. And as soon as the war ended, he approached the liberators and volunteered to track down the Nazi criminals himself. The props for the rest of his life were falling into place; only one pivotal piece of the action had yet to be set into motion.

In the winter of 1946, the American rabbi who served as the Jewish chaplain of the DP camp in which Wiesenthal had been interned asked him to join him on a harrowing expedition. The army had learned that a castle in Bavaria had been designated by the Nazis as a "Museum to the Extinct Jewish Race," and that it overflowed with Judaica and prayer books looted from Jewish homes all over Europe. The army had asked the chaplain, an expert on Jewish matters, to inspect the premises and report on his findings. But he feared he would find it too traumatic to go through the collection alone, he told Wiesenthal; moreover, it was too daunting a task. Would Wiesenthal accompany him?

The two men grew pensive as they entered the castle and surveyed the scene before them. They gasped as their eyes absorbed the relics of a vanished life. A veritable warehouse of Judaica surrounded them: ceremonial and ritual objects, phylacteries, paintings, silver, Torahs, prayer shawls, holy books, and more. They fell silent as they contemplated the ghosts of the absent owners that swirled around them: the proud young bar mitzvah boy who would never recite the *kiddush* blessing over his prized silver wine cup; the blushing bride who would never see the flames dance on her Sabbath candelabra in which her beloved's face was reflected; the elderly grandfather whose tender kiss the velvet Torah scroll would never know anymore. All of them had been eradicated, ground into dust. Perversely, their possessions, mere objects, lived on . . . in mute testimony, in quiet rebuke.

The two walked the rooms together, Wiesenthal and the chaplain, brushing the objects lightly with their fingertips, touching them reverentially, murmuring exclamations in hushed tones; and then they drifted apart, exploring separately. Simon was in fact far from the chaplain's side when he suddenly heard him scream.

When he reached the chaplain, his head was bowed,

tears streaming down his face. Wordlessly, he handed Simon the object in his hand. It was a simple Jewish prayer book of a type common to Europe and to the era. Why had it elicited such a strong emotional response from the chaplain, Simon wondered.

Silently, the chaplain pointed to the inscription inside.

It bore a woman's handwriting.

She had written: "I am begging whoever finds this prayer book to help avenge the deaths of the Jews of Europe."

She had signed her full name at the bottom of the inscription, but the name meant nothing to Simon. It did, however, bear meaning for the chaplain.

"My sister," he said.

He had made it out of Europe in time, but his sister had been ensnared in Hitler's net. In America, he had desperately sought news of her, but there had been none. Until now.

She had apparently written the inscription in quiet desperation just moments before her death. "They are coming," she had scribbled hastily. "The murderers are among us. . . . I hear them in the next house. Avenge our deaths!"

The ghosts rattled their sabers and the room roared with their silent groaning. For the chaplain, the discovery was a message from the grave. For Simon Wiesenthal, it provided the mission that charged his life.

The Murderers Among Us became the title of his first book on Nazi war criminals—a living memorial to the woman whose words haunted his nights and galvanized his days, whose clarion call for justice became his raison d'être.

"As a body of water clearly reflects one's face, so too does one heart reflect another," an ancient Jewish proverb states, articulating the belief that feelings are always mutual. But in the case of Larry Davis* and Lily Jacobs,* it just wasn't so. Larry was hopelessly smitten with Lily, but his strong emotions weren't reciprocated. Lily liked Larry well enough—in fact, she regarded him as one of her very best friends. But romance? "He was totally in love with me, but all that time I never really knew," Lily says.

The two had met in study hall at Bexley High School in Columbus, Ohio, in 1957, where the student body was predominantly Jewish. They connected right away, and found they were kindred spirits from the start. "I told him all my problems," says Lily. "He would walk me home from school every day, and we'd watch *American Bandstand* together on TV, and then we'd spend hours every night on the phone."

Larry was convinced that he had found the love of his life—but Lily had another boyfriend in school, and it was he who was the focus of her thoughts. Stalwart, Larry remained Lily's faithful confidant and listened attentively to the details of her ongoing relationship with Steve Arnold, even while his own heart ached. They never talked outright about the discrepancy in their feelings toward each other.

After high school graduation, the two went their separate ways. Lily went to college in Philadelphia, while Larry went to a local college in Columbus. Larry thought about Lily continuously and contemplated traveling to Philadelphia to visit her, but then reconsidered. *What's the use?* he thought in despair. *Her feelings for me are never going to change.*

Three years later, in 1964, Lily was engaged to someone else. When Larry saw her together with her fiancé at a movie theater in Columbus, he turned away. He almost left because he was so upset.

Lily and her husband moved to Wichita, Kansas, but returned to Columbus often to visit her parents. Once, when Lily was back home walking down the street pushing a baby carriage, Larry drove by. When he saw Lily, his heart broke, and he pushed the gas pedal to go faster. He sped by without stopping to say hello.

It took many years for Larry to nurse his broken heart, but ultimately, he became reconciled to the fact that Lily would never be his. He tried to push her out of his head and heart and fashion a new life for himself. He moved to Atlanta, where he finally got married at the age of thirty-one.

In Atlanta, Larry worked hard and raised a family, becoming a prosperous businessman and devoted father. He succeeded in achieving many of the goals toward which he has aspired. There was one, however, that he failed to attain. He still could not get Lily entirely out of his heart. From time to time, he would call Carol, Lily's best friend from Columbus, to check up on Lily and see how she was doing.

Lily had a good marriage and four wonderful children, Carol would tell Larry when he called for news. But soon things in Lily's life began to change dramatically for the worse. When Lily's oldest daughter turned fourteen, she became ill. The diagnosis was cancer. Four years later she was dead, and the family was devastated. Lily, in particular, felt that her life was over. "I didn't laugh or smile for the next ten years," she remembers. "I was sure that I would never experience happiness again in my lifetime. But I also felt strongly that I had to keep going for the sake of my other three children, so I kept pushing myself."

But despite her best attempts, Lily could no longer keep her floundering marriage alive. "Eighty percent of marriages that experience the trauma of the death of a child end in divorce," she explains. "Ours was one of those statistics. There had just been too much stress and pain over the last four years. Our marriage literally could not bear it."

Lily kept going, but her life was joyless. She tried to incorporate a sense of normalcy into her life so that her children would remain healthy and functioning. Lily was fortunate in that she had a coterie of dedicated friends in Wichita, who bolstered her with their love and support.

One of these close friends was Jossie. "We had gone

through a lot together—Jossie's two divorces, the death of my daughter, then my own divorce. Jossie was more than a friend, she was family. And her mother and father—who visited Wichita often—became my surrogate parents, too. We were all very close."

In August, 1994, Jossie decided to throw a gala fiftieth wedding anniversary party for her parents in their hometown of Atlanta, and she asked Lily to come. "I was very hesitant, very reluctant," Lily recalls. "First of all, I was in financial straits, and the cost of the airplane ticket and hotel stay was prohibitive. I had also given up on life, and psychologically was not in the best state of mind. You don't want to go to parties when you feel so blue. But I reasoned, if, God forbid, Jossie's parents died, I would certainly go to their funeral, so why shouldn't I partici-pate in a joyous occasion? It's really a *mitzvah*, I thought."

From childhood on, Lily's father had always told her, "Do what you know is right . . . even if it requires extra effort or sacrifice." Lily had internalized this message well. "After wrestling with myself for a long time, I decided to go. It was really the right thing to do."

At the party, a typical busybody type pounced on Lily with glee. "So, where are you from?" she began to chitchat. When Lily mentioned that she originally hailed from Columbus, the woman's eyes widened. "Oh, do you know Larry Davis?" she asked. When Lily mentioned that they had been best friends in high school, the woman exclaimed, "Well, do you know that he lives right here in Atlanta?"

Lily expressed surprise, but little interest. She was still too depressed to have any desire to revive old friendships.

But if Lily was less than avid, the woman was downright fervent about pursuing business that was not her own. True to form, the meddlesome gossip picked up the phone the next morning and called Larry. "Guess what?" she trilled in excitement. "I met an old friend of yours last night. Lily."

Lily may have been dispassionate about the news, but Larry was elated to hear that his old friend was in town. "Where is she?" he asked excitedly.

The busybody was prepared: She had managed to extract that information from Lily the previous night as well, so she was able to supply Larry with the name of the hotel.

Within seconds, Larry was on the phone. But Lily's line was busy. Larry called the hotel operator and begged him to interrupt Lily's call, but the operator refused. Then, unable to restrain his excitement, Larry drove down to the hotel to beg in person; but the operator remained adamant. Larry returned home, and finally got Lily on the phone.

"Hi, this is Larry!" his hearty voice boomed with excitement.

"Oh, hi," Lily responded dully.

"I'd like to come over and say hello," he said.

"Oh, no, that's not possible," she replied indifferently. "I'm meeting some people for brunch in a little while."

"Well, just for a few minutes then," he wheedled. "Please? I'll meet you in the lobby."

He was fifty-five years old, but he showed up in jeans, a T-shirt, a helmet, and a Harley motorcycle. Her friends thought he was cool—but Lily was unresponsive. They spoke for a few minutes, but Lily remained chilly and distant. She was careful about the details she shared with him. "I was sure that he was happily married, so I was inhibited in what I told him about my life."

But Larry's marriage had, in fact, ended a long time before. It had been in trouble from the start, and although he and his wife had tried counseling for many years, they hadn't been able to make the marriage work. By the time Larry met Lily, he had been officially separated from his wife for many months.

The meeting was, for Lily, uneventful, but for Larry, it had been momentous. He still retained strong feelings for her—the same feelings he had always had.

A few days later, Larry called Lily at her home in Wichita. "I just wanted you to know how nice it was to see you again," he said.

"I have to go," Lily replied curtly. She didn't know why he was calling her, but she was sure that his behavior was inappropriate for a married man.

But Larry refused to be deterred as he had been

thirty-five years back. This time he would be persistent and express the feelings he had squelched for so many decades.

The next week Larry called again, and this time he told her that he was in the middle of divorce proceedings. Relieved that his intentions were not dishonorable, Lily relaxed, and they began conversing on the phone for hours at a time, slipping back into old and familiar rhythms. "It was just like when we were back in high school," Lily says.

In more ways than one. They had reverted to the original pattern, the first model. In an exact repetition of the scenario of earlier years, Larry was wild about Lily, but she still regarded him as a long-lost friend and nothing more. She was happy to have him back in her life again, "but it certainly wasn't part of my plan to fall in love with him."

Lily refused to see Larry until his divorce was final. But that didn't keep the inevitable from happening over the phone. What had taken thirty-five years to develop suddenly burst into full bloom. It had taken all this time, but it had grown, matured, and ripened like grapes nurtured carefully on the vine. And, like old wine, it was very sweet. Lily had finally fallen in love with Larry, who had never fallen out of love with her at all.

The two got married eight months later on April 20, 1996 ("When you're in your fifties, life doesn't wait for you," Lily explains) — thirty-nine years after they first met in school. "And today I am so happy and feel so lucky, I just can't believe it," she says.

Last year, Lily accompanied Larry to their high school class reunion, and no one there was surprised to see the two of them as husband and wife.

"People just assumed that we had always been together. And in a certain way, they were right."

In 1989, I was a member of a delegation of thirty-three men who traveled from Brooklyn to London to attend the wedding of our Rebbe's son, Naftali. We spent several days in the Hasidic enclave of Stamford Hill, participating in various wedding festivities, feeling privileged to be able to accord this honor to our spiritual master.

When the day arrived for us to return home, we stopped off at the Rebbe's home first for a formal leave-taking ceremony. We informed his *gabbai* (assistant) that we were on a tight schedule, and that we had to be at Heathrow Airport within two hours in order to catch our plane. The *gabbai* nodded his understanding and said genially: "There shouldn't be any problem. The Rebbe happens to be free right now; he slotted in this time just for you. I'll inform him that you're here, and I'm sure he will be able to see you immediately."

But when the *gabbai* returned from the Rebbe's study, he didn't make any attempt to usher us in. He wore a slight frown, as he said in a subdued voice, "The Rebbe says you should wait."

Although the *gabbai* had only moments before said that the Rebbe was free, we weren't puzzled or offended. We assumed the Rebbe was preparing for his audience with us by engaging in a meditative act or simple prayer. We were sure he would call us in momentarily. However, when a full half-hour elapsed, and we found ourselves still waiting in the anteroom, we began to get edgy. Someone went to summon the *gabbai* and inquire about the delay. "I'll go remind the Rebbe once more," he said promptly. "I'm sure he'll tell me to bring you in right away." But once again the *gabbai* emerged from the Rebbe's study with a perplexed look on his face. "I'm sorry," he shrugged, appearing awkward and embarrassed, "but the Rebbe says you still have to wait."

By now, we were beginning to get frantic. This was *very* uncharacteristic behavior on the part of the Rebbe, who was renowned for keeping his appointments punctually. Additionally, he was an extremely humble and modest person, who was most respectful of all of his followers' needs and would never willingly keep them waiting. What was most puzzling, however, was the fact that the *gabbai* had already reported to us that the Rebbe was alone in his study. So what was holding him back from seeing us immediately, we couldn't help but wonder?

"Excuse me," one of the Hasidim asked deferentially of the *gabbai*. "Is the Rebbe maybe . . . ill?"

The *gabbai* shook his head.

"Is he praying?"

"No!" answered the *gabbai* impatiently.

"So what is he doing in there?" another asked, a little impertinently.

The *gabbai* just shrugged his shoulders and left the room.

As soon as he left, everyone started whispering nervously. "I think we have no choice but to just get up and leave now," one man suggested. "If we don't we're going to miss our plane!"

"Don't even consider it!" remonstrated another. "The Rebbe would be terribly offended."

Almost everyone sided with the second man. There was just no way we could leave. We had to stay and hope we would make our plane.

When the *gabbai* finally ushered us into the Rebbe's office, we were greeted warmly by our Master, but no word of apology about the interminable delay issued from his lips. That, too, was puzzling, and not typical of our Rebbe at all. The Rebbe was known to be so respectful of other people's time that he had been heard to apologize profusely for keeping someone waiting for five minutes! He had kept *us* waiting for close to an hour, but he offered neither an explanation nor an excuse. Very strange, we all agreed.

The moment our audience with the Rebbe ended, we rushed into a waiting bus that had been chartered to drive us to the airport, and impolitely shouted at the flustered driver to drive fast, faster! Our exhortations, however, proved useless. We soon found ourselves snarled in a massive traffic jam encircling Heathrow, and our hopes of making the plane grew increasingly dim.

When we reached Heathrow, we were informed that the plane—the last one out to New York that day—had just taken off. We were devastated! Many of us were businessmen and had important business appointments set up for the next day; others among us had family weddings and bar mitzvahs to attend the following night. We felt frustrated, upset, and mad.

But an hour later, the words of lament had frozen on our lips and turned to fervent prayers of gratitude instead.

For the Pan Am plane that we had so regretted missing had just tragically blown up over Lockerbie, Scotland. The tragedy that had befallen the passengers was too terrible to comprehend.

We felt horror and anguish for those on board; we were mute with grief. At the same time, however, we couldn't help but be grateful to the Rebbe and the hand of God that had spared our lives.

*W*as it possible that just one year ago he had been part of a sprawling, boisterous, happy family of ten, and that now—one year later—he was the only one left? It seemed as if the memories he preserved belonged to a different time, a different place, and a vastly different person. He was not the same man he had been in 1944, before his universe had suddenly turned dark. In one short year, everything had changed, and the world as he recalled it was forever gone. This was as true for him as it was for countless thousand other survivors. Life, as he had once known it, had ceased to exist.

In 1944, before the war encroached upon Yugoslavia, seventeen-year-old Ernest Hollander had four sisters and three brothers, who comprised a tight-knit clan shepherded by warm and loving parents. But by 1945, every single one of them was gone, including his mother and father.

Ernest had been interned—together with his younger brother Alex and his father—at four of the bleakest concentration camps of the Nazi death machine: Auschwitz, Dachau, Bergen-Belsen, and Birkenau. He had watched as his father was shot and killed before his very eyes, and his brother had been murdered, too; but Ernest had survived, hoping that perhaps some of the others were still alive. But he soon discovered that he was the sole survivor of a household that had once spilled over with love, laughter, and life.

"I don't believe it . . . I can't believe it," Ernest tried to deny the reports as mere hearsay. "I have to know for sure."

Like thousands of other dazed and stricken survivors who struggled to find family after the war, Ernest tried to cut through the bureaucratic labyrinth of Red Cross organizations, displaced persons camps, and Jewish social service agencies. Throughout his search he checked bulletin boards where names of survivors were posted alongside names of the deceased, ever hopeful that he would find an answer.

Ernest quickly learned that the Jewish grapevine still operated efficiently. The reports about his family proved to be true, after all. With the help of various officials, Ernest was able to determine the fate of his family members and corroborate the initial accounts he had originally discounted as rumors and lies. Now they were hard facts: confirmed, authenticated, stamped, and sealed. His three younger sisters had been gassed in Auschwitz together with their mother; and another sister and brother had been lost in different camps. Soon all his siblings were accounted for, with the exception of one: his older brother Herschel. Sucked into the maelstrom of the Holocaust, Herschel had simply vanished without a trace. No one knew whether he was dead or alive.

Ernest chose to believe that his brother had

survived and went looking for him. He crisscrossed Europe several times, searching for Herschel in refugee camps, in schools set up for survivors—even in his old home town. And when his exhaustive searches yielded no results, Ernest expanded the hunt to include Israel as well, a country to which so many survivors had fled. But here his attempts also proved futile. Eventually, Ernest acknowledged defeat, conceding that in all likelihood his brother, too, was gone. With a heavy heart, Ernest emigrated to America, and settled in Oakland, California, a suburb of San Francisco.

Ernest began life anew, but he never forgot the horrors of the Holocaust. "Never again!" he vowed, promising himself that he would do everything in his power to eradicate evil in his lifetime. In California, he kept that pledge. He became extremely active in both general and Jewish community affairs, emerging as a force to be reckoned with. His leadership skills particularly benefited his pet project: Holocaust education. For over forty years, Ernest dedicated himself to traveling across California to deliver lectures at more than 200 public schools a year. He believed that the root causes of hatred, intolerance, prejudice, and anti-Semitism could be eliminated with the proper education of the masses, beginning with its children and teenagers. He made a name for himself and became a much sought-after speaker.

In 1992, the very enterprising producers of the

Montel Williams television show—then based in California—conceived an inventive idea: an on-air debate between a neo-Nazi and a Holocaust historian. The producers readily found a neo-Nazi willing to come on board, but a Holocaust historian who was also a survivor himself was harder to locate. Some eligible candidates were simply gun shy, while others were loath to share a platform with a human being who stood for hatred. In desperation, the producers put in calls to a plethora of Jewish organizations throughout California: *Did anyone know of a Holocaust historian/survivor who would be willing to debate a neo-Nazi on television?*

"Ernest Hollander," everybody said.

Ernest was excited at the prospects such a televised debate could offer. "Lecturing at public schools each year affords me the opportunity to positively influence thousands of children and teenagers," he reasoned, "but with national television, my message can reach hundreds of thousands of adults as well. How can I turn away such a chance?"

Ernest agreed to do the television show in the spirit of idealism and activism. *Who knows how many lives might change as a result?* he thought. Ernest had no inkling that the person for whom the greatest change would occur would be . . . himself.

A New Yorker named Ziga would bring it about. A recent émigré from Yugoslavia, Ziga worked a long day shift that ended at ten o'clock in the evening. His wife, a health care practitioner, worked long hours as well; she had the night shift from six in the evening until six in the morning. During the four-hour interval between his wife's departure to work and Ziga's return home, a babysitter was enlisted to care for their infant. The arrangement had functioned smoothly until now, but on this particular evening, a minor crisis had erupted: The babysitter had suddenly called in sick, and Ziga's wife could not find a substitute on such short notice. She was worried that she would jeopardize her job if she missed any more work. Ziga, on the other hand, appeared securely entrenched in his, and had more leeway with his boss. His wife called Ziga in a panic: *Could he leave work four hours early and come home to babysit?*

Ziga came home early to remedy the situation. Suddenly, he found he had an evening to himself. The night was young, the baby was sound asleep, and he himself was still uncommonly alert and wakeful. Absently, Ziga flicked on the television set and randomly began surfing the channels. Nothing appealed to him and he proceeded to punch the buttons on the remote with continued disinterest. But when Channel 9 flashed on the screen, Ziga's attention was immediately riveted. He stared at the television in mingled shock and disbelief and emitted a low whistle of surprise. "Now whatever is Herschel Hollander doing on the *Montel Williams Show?*" he asked in stupefaction.

Ziga and Herschel Hollander went back many years.

Ziga had grown up in the same apartment building in Krakuujevik, Yugoslavia, where Herschel Hollander had made his home for more than forty years. The older man had taken an interest in young Ziga and befriended him. Sure that Herschel was still ensconced in Yugoslavia, Ziga was startled to see his friend's visage, right there in front of him, on an American program.

"I can't believe he would come to the States and not call me to say hello," Ziga sniffed, somewhat insulted.

"Well, I'll call him then," he reconsidered, and picked up the phone to dial the *Montel Williams Show.*

"Sorry, sir," an unyielding female voice answered his inquiries. "The guests are not in the studio now. The show was prerecorded. And I'm not allowed to give out their numbers, anyway."

"But I'm begging you . . . Herschel Hollander is a good friend of mine from Yugoslavia!" Ziga entreated.

"Sir, you've made a mistake. The guest on tonight's show is named *Ernest* and he's American."

"That's impossible," Ziga protested. "I know my friend."

"Well, your friend must have a double then. It's a case of mistaken identity. Good bye."

Ziga was baffled. The man on the *Montel Williams Show* looked like Herschel Hollander, spoke like Herschel Hollander, and his last name was, in fact, Hollander. Did doubles really exist?

How could there be so many similarities between the

two men with no commonality whatsoever? This was the question Ziga was still puzzling over a few weeks later when he flew to Yugoslavia for a visit with family and friends.

"You know, Herschel," he told his friend when he visited him in his home, "there is a man in America who looks like you, talks like you, and acts like you. His name is Hollander, too."

"And what is his first name?" Herschel asked his friend.

"Ernest."

"My brother," Herschel whispered. "My brother who all these years I believed was dead. Can he really be alive?"

He picked up the phone to call the *Montel Williams Show*.

The producers were almost as excited as he to learn of the miracle spurred on by their show. They said they'd be glad to give Herschel his brother's phone number, and they suggested the actual reunion take place on the show. Herschel agreed.

In October 1992, Ernest Hollander returned to the *Montel Williams Show* to reunite with his brother Herschel, whom he had not seen for fifty-two years. Although by that point the two had spoken to each other numerous times over the phone, this was the first time that they were meeting in person. Their dramatic, poignant, and heart-rending reunion—exactly as the producers had envisioned it—took place on national TV.

Herschel remained in America for over a year to become reacquainted with Ernest, and Ernest later traveled to Yugoslavia to spend several months with Herschel. "I had six wonderful years with my brother until he died in 1999," Ernest says with a catch in his voice. "After a lifetime apart, six years was much too short, but whatever time I had with my brother I consider a great blessing."

Ernest had originally appeared on the *Montel Williams Show* with the objective of puncturing the misconceptions that helped pave the way for the Holocaust and that underlie current anti-Semitism. How could he possibly have known that this same television appearance would pave the way for his own personal miracle as well?

"Everything hinged on Ziga," he recalls. "If he hadn't come home early that night, when the babysitter called in sick, my reunion with my brother would never have happened."

I had watched roses blooming outside my kitchen window for fifteen years. I loved those magnificent beauties, but I never cut them to bring indoors. Strange as it may seem, they lived only a few days each season before the petals began falling to the ground and the flowers disappeared.

One summer, we had a drought and my beautiful flowers did not bloom at all, since roses need an abundance of water to grow. In addition, I had neglected to water them because I was consumed with sadness. My beloved mother—my friend, my teacher, my confidante—had been terminally ill for months and I was heartbroken and helpless. Finally, one scorching day in June, the inevitable happened; my dear mother died.

On the day of the funeral, the ground was parched as the temperature soared to 100 degrees. When I returned home, I was greeted outside my kitchen window by the biggest, most magnificent red rose I'd ever seen. Not only was it exquisite but it was huge! Such a perfect specimen could never have grown to such greatness unnoticed. I am as positive now as I was then that the rose did not exist before my mother's funeral. It appeared, as if by magic, on that bush outside my kitchen window just after my mother was laid to rest.

All who came to pay their respects during that week after my mother's death marveled at the size and beauty of the rose. I looked out my window every morning expecting to see red petals on the ground, but the rose remained intact. Not one petal fell from it during that week or the next, or even during the entire month after my mother's death.

On one of those hot, dry, windless days, as my son, my daughter, and I sat outside on the patio, the rose and its branch began to bounce and wave wildly before our very eyes. We immediately realized that no other branches were moving; no wind was blowing; no blades of grass were stirring. We were all in awe—afraid to breathe for fear of erasing the enchanting scene. And then one of my children quietly said, "I think Gram is telling us something. Let's try to understand."

When I described the incident to a friend who is a rabbi, he immediately explained that miracles happen to us every day—that God often sends us messages through Nature—but that we must be open to receive them. He told me very matter-of-factly: "Of course, that rose is a messenger from your mother. She's telling you not to worry because she's doing fine now in a place of beauty and greatness."

And so it was that the rose continued to live and shed beauty and generate memories. When it was finally time for it to depart after eight comforting months, the petals did not fall one by one as in the past. The rose slowly shriveled up, turned black, and remained completely intact until it was dead. There it stayed on the branch until my gardener trimmed the rosebush and cut it off.

I had forgotten to tell him the story of my beloved mother and her special message in that miraculous rose. I often ponder what would have happened to the rose had my gardener let Nature take its course.

—Gail Raab

*I*n October 1995, I served as scholar in residence for the Jewish community of São Paulo, Brazil. During my stay, I was graciously hosted by the Safras, a prominent and distinguished family, who couldn't do enough for me. One day, they insisted on showing me the sights and escorted me to various tourist attractions. One of the most popular of these spots just happened to be a racetrack. When I confessed to my host that this represented a brand-new experience for me, he urged me to place a bet on a horse to get into the spirit of the race.

I approached the cashier, studied the names of the horses in the next race (which were in Portuguese), and, heeding my intuition, chose one instantly. Although I don't understand the language, the configuration of letters appealed to me, and the name seemed pretty. My instincts told me that I had just selected the winner.

"Number two, please," I requested in a clear, firm voice.

After I returned to my seat, I realized that the cashier had made a mistake. He didn't speak English well, and he had obviously misunderstood my request. He had given me number four instead.

Ordinarily, I probably would have been passive about the error, shrugged my shoulders indifferently, and not made any undue fuss. But this time, I was convinced that number two was my ticket to untold riches, and I didn't want to cede my opportunity so quickly. So I got up from my seat and returned to the cashier's window.

"I'm so sorry to disturb you," I said softly, "but you gave me the wrong number. I asked for two and you gave me four instead."

My apologetic manner was unfortunately not matched by his. He glared at me angrily and refused to exchange the ticket.

"I give you number you ask," he insisted. "No can change."

I dug in my heels and became as intractable as he.

"I'm sorry, but it's your mistake. I know what I asked for and I asked for number two."

"You ask for number four, and that's what I give you."

We locked horns and argued loudly. The line behind me grew long with impatient customers. Finally, the cashier caved in and exchanged my ticket. Flushed with my success, I returned to the bench, holding the number two ticket triumphantly in my hand.

But not for long.

For the winner of the race was none other than . . . number four.

And since the odds of that particular horse winning had been extremely low, those who placed their bets on number four went home that day with a huge windfall.

A windfall that, alas, I was not to share in.

Thunderstruck by this turn of events, I turned to my

host and urgently asked: "What's the name of the winning horse?"

He murmured something in Portuguese, unintelligible to me.

"No, not in Portuguese," I said. "In English. What does the horse's name mean in English?"

"With God's help."

"Excuse me?" I asked.

"That's the horse's name," my host replied. "The horse's name is 'With God's help.'"

I groaned. It was not the *cashier* who had made the mistake, it was *I*.

God had thrown a gift into my hands and I had given it away. God had pushed me in a certain direction, and I hadn't understood His gentle "nudge" at all. And my mistake had been costly.

Today, when something like this happens, I don't question it, and I don't challenge it. I "go with the flow," as the popular maxim says, and see where the mistake will lead me.

Because sometimes it's not a "mistake" at all, but a blessing in disguise.

—*Rabbi Benjamin Blech*

*W*ith an easygoing, friendly disposition and a penchant for performing charitable deeds, Edith Kleinman* always said yes to life. Even though she was a relative newcomer to the small village of Heveningen, Holland (having emigrated there as a young bride from Switzerland), her reputation as a tenderhearted soul grew quickly. So it came as no surprise when the Christian constable of the village, Herr Schleider,* approached Edith one morning in 1939 and asked if she could do an enormous favor for his family.

"I understand that you had a baby recently," he said, as she welcomed him into her home. "I don't know if you're aware of this, but my wife also just gave birth . . . to triplets."

Edith Kleinman murmured her surprise and congratulations.

"As you can imagine, my wife and I are filled with joy, but are also quite . . . overwhelmed. And we are faced with a difficult problem. My wife does not have enough milk to suckle all three babies. She barely has enough for one. The doctor has told me that the infants are very malnourished; they're starving, he says. Many people in town have told me that you are a very kind woman. . . . I know this is a lot to ask of you . . . but would you be able to serve as wet nurse for two of the triplets? . . . I will pay you, of course," he added hastily.

"Oh, no!" Edith protested vigorously. "I will absolutely not accept payment from you. It will be my privilege to help your babies get a good start in life. How could I possibly say no to such a request? Of course, I'll do it!"

As was typical of her, Edith Kleinman had once again said yes with no forethought, afterthought, or regret.

She nursed those babies for nine months, and they grew strong and robust.

"I will never forget what you've done for my children," the constable said gratefully when the infants were ready to be weaned. "If it weren't for you, they could have died."

Three years later, the Kleinmans were packing for their yearly trip to Switzerland when they heard a loud knock on the door. It was the constable, whom they had not seen for many months. He appeared tense, nervous, and afraid. His eyes roamed the street anxiously before he slipped in, almost stealthily, through their front door.

He plunged right in with the purpose of his call.

"I hear that you spend the Passover holidays every year with your family in Switzerland," he said.

"Yes," Edith murmured in assent. "We do."

"When you leave this year, take along some extra suitcases," he whispered. "Pack your most valuable and precious possessions, those that are among your most beloved, sentimental, or costly. And go, ostensibly for the holiday—but don't come back."

"Wh-wh-what?" Edith asked in confusion. "I don't understand . . ."

"I've joined the Nazis," the constable explained, "and really, I should not be here at all. But how can I forget what you did for my children? . . . You may tell—and take along—your extended family, but you mustn't share this with anyone else. A sudden mass departure would be noted and stopped. I am sorry I can't elaborate, but trust me and heed my warning. Leave and don't come back."

As the constable stole out the door, he glanced over his shoulder and whispered to the Kleinmans: "My debt to you is paid."

On the seventh day of Passover, Hitler's troops marched into Holland, ambushing the Jewish citizenry, who were taken by surprise. Unprepared for the sudden onslaught, most Dutch Jews were unable to escape and found themselves ensnared in the Nazis' vicious web. Almost all of Holland's Jews perished in the war, with only a minuscule number surviving the Holocaust.

But the Kleinmans, safe in Switzerland when the invasion took place, were able to procure visas to the United States, where they found haven and a new life.

"Down the road, you can never really imagine how your destiny will play out," muses a reflective ninety-year-old Edith Kleinman today. "Serving as the infants' wet nurse just seemed like the right thing to do. How could I ever know that when I was saying yes to their lives, I was saying it to my own, as well."

*M*oishe was the type of guy to whom no woman could be indifferent. His refreshing honesty—which sometimes bordered on the edge of brusque—charmed many, alienated others. Consequently, there were months when his calendar was crammed with dates, and alternately, weeks when Saturday nights were devoted to solo trips to the laundromat. These were the interludes that the forty-two-year-old liked to refer to as "the dry spells."

In July 1999, the dry spells had escalated to a full-fledged drought, and Moishe was propelled to do something he usually avoided like the plague: attend a singles weekend. Moishe felt uncomfortable with "the scene" and claimed that these weekends were a waste of time. Still, he was forty-two years old and unmarried, and he was ready to work hard to find his soul mate.

So, off to the Rye Town Hilton he dragged himself unwillingly one Friday to participate in a Shabbat Nachamu (a particularly festive Sabbath in the Jewish calendar) weekend sponsored by the Association of Orthodox Jewish Scientists. His hopes were not high.

But over the course of the weekend, his attention kept straying to one particular young lady who sparkled as she talked and smiled often. Many single women of a certain age, he had found, had long ago lost their luster and become bitter. He understood their disappointment, and fought bitterness himself, but it was still hard to countenance in others. This woman, however, seemed to possess no bitterness whatsoever, despite the fact that she, too, appeared likely to be in her early forties. She was friendly, warm, and alive. He decided to make a stab at chatting her up.

Summoning his courage, Moishe sauntered over to her in his usual debonair way, and learned that her name was Evelyn. Close up, she was as charming as she had seemed from a distance. She was a great conversationalist, warm and sweet. His spirits began to brighten. Maybe the weekend wouldn't be a total washout after all.

Moishe could never put on airs or make a pretense of being somebody he wasn't. So he was his usual self, which tended to mean different things to different people. Some—kinder and gentler souls—would describe Moishe's "usual self" as candid, frank, and straightforward; others would disagree and call him too blunt.

Evelyn herself minced no words in her assessment of Moishe's personality. In her opinion, she told him flat-out, he was quite simply . . . "obnoxious."

Moishe was crushed. He had just asked Evelyn for her phone number, assuming that his feelings for her were reciprocated.

They weren't.

He couldn't believe it. He had been sure she was as excited about him as he was about her.

She wasn't.

He had really enjoyed their conversations over the weekend, he told her, and thought they had established a wonderful rapport.

"What rapport?" she asked, incredulous.

Moishe returned home, dejected. Finally, he had met a woman who he had believed appreciated him for what he was. But "obnoxious" didn't quite seem . . . appreciative enough.

The characterization stung. What had he done to spark such virulence, such antipathy in Evelyn? She seemed downright hostile toward him. *Sorry, but I just can't stand you,* is basically what she had said.

Moishe soldiered on. Over the next several months, he was fixed up on countless blind dates with eligible young women, many of whom did indeed appreciate his wit, his candor, his sense of honor and integrity. But he, on his part, found them somehow lacking.

In March 2000, he mustered his strength, marshaled his forces, and sallied forth to an unfamiliar Brooklyn neighborhood where a singles party was being held. A series of mishaps made him late, and then he got lost, and soon he felt a tension headache pounding at his temples. He began to wonder if he shouldn't forget the party and head back home. His nervousness was compounded by the fact that he couldn't find a parking space.

Moishe circled the streets in a futile quest for a spot, and had all but called it quits, when he saw the rear headlights of a parked car suddenly blaze up in illumination—a signal that it was about to leave. Breathing a sigh of relief, he quickly drew up behind and waited for the car to pull out.

It didn't move.

He counted: one minute, two minutes, three. What was the matter with the driver? How long did it take to find your keys and belt yourself in?

Soon, his patience began to wear thin.

He rolled down his car window, honked his horn, and bellowed out in his typical genteel way: "Are you moving out or what?"

The other driver peeked out the window, took a long, hard look at him and said: "Well, now that I see who wants my spot . . . I'm not budging!"

It was Evelyn.

Moishe's jaw dropped.

"I . . . I can't b-believe this," he stammered in wonder. "I just thought about you today."

"Try that line on somebody else, buddy," she said, rolling her eyes in disbelief.

"No really," he said, "I mean it. . . . I may be obnoxious, but I'm not a liar. Really, I just thought about you only a little while ago."

The two started arguing through their open car windows, Moishe professing his sincerity, Evelyn her skepticism. Moishe had indeed thought about Evelyn that day with yearning and regret, so when she continued to express disbelief, his fuse blew. Angrily, he got out of his car to stand alongside hers and argue with her *outside*. Then he determinedly climbed into her car and argued with her *inside*. And three months later . . . not a small miracle but a *big* one . . . they were engaged.

It's one week before the wedding now, and the time has come to tell their tale. I know it intimately, having heard it recounted at many different venues . . . engagement parties, wedding showers, and family dinners. You see, Moishe is my brother, the one I thought was destined to eternal bachelorhood. But if there are two lessons to be learned from this tale, they are: (1) never give up on anyone, and (2) if someone tells you with vehemence and vigor that they found their date to be absolutely, utterly, completely, irrevocably, and unequivocally *obnoxious* . . . get out your dancing shoes!

—*Yitta Halberstam*

*I*n a small, makeshift synagogue not far from the Twin Towers, Orthodox Jewish professionals regularly meet early each morning for daily prayer services. Usually there is no problem rounding up a *minyan* (quorum of ten men required to pray) and the cramped quarters often overflow with worshipers. But on the morning of September 11th, there was an uncommon dearth of available men. Perhaps they had decided to remain that morning at their resident *shuls* for the important *selichos* services that precede the High Holidays. Or, perhaps, they were participating in the *shloshim* (one month anniversary) memorial services for the Jews who had been killed in the Grand Canyon helicopter crash. Two hundred men who worked in the World Trade Center, were, in fact, late to work that morning because of their participation in that *shloshim* service. But whatever the reason, the congregants were faced with a problem: Only nine men were present, and time was marching on. These were serious men, professionals, and all had to be at their desks at the World Trade Center well before 9:00 A.M.

"What should we do?" they asked each other, impatiently tapping their wristwatches, as they paced the floors. "This situation hasn't happened in ages! Where *is* everybody?"

"I'm sure a tenth man will come along soon," someone

else soothed. "We have to be patient."

The men waited, restless and tense. Some of them were already running late. Finally, when they had all but given up and were going to resort to individual prayer (instead of the preferred communal one), an old man whom nobody had ever seen before shuffled in the door.

"Did you *daven* (pray) yet?" he asked, looking around at the group.

"No, sir!" one shouted jubilantly. "We've been waiting for *you!*"

"Wonderful," the elderly man responded. "I have to say *kaddish* (a special prayer recited on the *yahrzeitt*, the anniversary of a close family member's death) for my father and I have to *daven* before the *omed* (lead the prayer services). I'm so glad that you didn't start yet."

Under normal circumstances, the men would have asked the gentleman polite questions: what was his name, where was he from, how did he come to their obscure *shul*? By now, however, they were frantic to start and decided to bypass protocol. They hastily handed the man a *siddur* (prayer book), hoping he would prove himself to be the Speedy Gonzalez of *daveners* (prayers). The old man proved to be anything but.

He seemed to rifle the pages of the *siddur* in agonizingly slow motion. Indeed, every gesture and movement that the man made seemed deliberately unhurried, protracted, and prolonged. The worshipers were respectful but definitely on *shpilkes* (pins and needles) to get to work.

"*Oy!*" someone smacked his forehead in frustration. "Are we going to be late!"

That's when they heard the first explosion: the horrible blast that would forever shake their souls. They ran outside and saw the smoke, the chaos, the screaming crowds, the apocalypse that lay before them.

It should have been us. After the initial shock and horror, consciousness dawned upon them quickly. They realized they had been rescued from the jaws of death. Each and every one of them worked in the Twin Towers. Each and every one of them was supposed to be there before nine. Had it not been for the elderly man and his slow-motion *schacharis* (morning services), they probably would have been killed.

They turned to thank him, this mystery man who had saved their lives. They wanted to hug him in effusive gratitude and find out his name and where he had come from on that fateful morning.

But they'll never know the answers to these questions that nag at them to this day—when they turned around to embrace him, the man was gone, his identity forever a mystery.

*M*y husband of blessed memory, Rabbi Meshulem Jungreis, was a man of great kindness and spirituality. His good deeds and charity encompassed all of God's creations. There was not a man, woman, or child—Jew and non-Jew alike—who crossed his path who did not become the beneficiary of a kind word, a benevolent act, a generous gift. He was the epitome of goodness. Everyone who met him felt blessed.

When we first moved to our new home in North Woodmere, Long Island, in the 1960s, my husband noticed a little lake across the street that was fenced in. A nature lover, he was enchanted by the idyllic scene it presented—its calm and tranquil waters, the wildflowers growing at its edges, the lush foliage of the trees that bordered its circumference. He took particular delight in making the acquaintance of its yearlong residential population—a platoon of ducks that honked noisily at his arrival. He was charmed. From that day forward, the ducks, too, joined the ranks of the recipients of my husband's largesse.

My husband became a regular—almost daily— visitor to the lake, bringing bread to feed the ducks, who soon began to recognize him. He took our children along with him, to teach them about the need to be kind to all living things and to demonstrate our interconnectedness. The children would squeal with pleasure and excitement as their chubby little hands threw the chunks of bread across the fence and the ducks dived for them in the water. Later, when the children got married and had children of their own, my husband continued the ritual. Only now he was accompanied by our grandchildren, who were as enthralled by the experience as their parents had been nearly two decades before.

My husband never forgot the ducks, even when he was ill. Until his untimely death in 1996, he remained constant to their needs—and a constant visitor to the lake. He fed them—and generations of their offspring— for more than thirty years.

In North Woodmere, where my husband had served both as pulpit rabbi and as chaplain of the Nassau County Police Department, he was accorded a funeral worthy of a head of state. Although the police force was mostly composed of non-Jews, over the years the officers had learned to love and respect my husband, and to look to him for spiritual guidance. When he died, every single man and woman on the force came out to pay their respects in what turned out to be a full ceremonial procession. Police helicopters whirled overhead as the police marched slowly down the streets of North Woodmere, joined by thousands of Jewish mourners. Part of North Woodmere had been cordoned off by the police, so the cortege of mourners was able to walk its narrow lanes, wider roads, and busy boulevards unimpeded. But when the procession approached my home, it suddenly came to a complete and abrupt halt.

The columns of people in the back couldn't understand why the throngs in front had unexpectedly stopped moving forward. Patient but curious, figures stepped out of line and faces peered ahead to find the cause of the problem. And when they did, a murmur of awe and wonder rippled through the crowd, like the bread that had been cast on the water so many years before.

For there, lined up across the road, in a procession of their own that stretched from the lake to my home on the other side of the street, was a long column of ducks that had closed ranks, standing in solemnity and silence. How had they broken out of the barricade that had enclosed them all these years? The fence used by the county to protect their enclosure appeared undamaged and intact; during all those decades the ducks had never before attempted to breach it.

Yet there they were, standing before us, motionless and still, and as we gazed on them spellbound, the murmur in our midst swelled.

I remembered how in the promise of springtime, the pathos of fall, the extravagance of summer, the desolation of winter, how in all the countless seasons that had measured off his life . . . my husband had never forgotten the ducks and their need. I saw his figure hunched over the fence as he bent to throw the chunks of challah and crusts of bread from brown paper bags, battered buckets, plastic containers. None of God's creations had been too small to escape his notice during his lifetime, and now, in his death, they had come to bear witness.

For as unlikely as it seemed, as mysterious and inexplicable a cosmic puzzle as it was, I knew in my heart that there was only one conceivable explanation for the unprecedented presence of the ducks on the road that fateful day.

Like their human counterparts, they were there for the funeral and to pay their respects.

In gratitude and remembrance, they had come to bid their benefactor a final farewell.

—*Rebetzin Esther Jungreis*

*H*ow *would my parents pay for my college education?*

That question, I learned years later, dominated their thoughts in 1968 when I, their oldest child, was a senior in high school.

My family was middle-class, with no extra money for the thousands of dollars that tuition and books and other sundries of university life required. Board for a dorm room out of town was out of the question; I would study locally.

Mom brought her worries to *her* mother, who lived above us in a two-family house on a modest side street. They would talk in broken English (Grandma's) and broken Yiddish (Mom's).

"Don't worry," Grandma would console Mom. "Steve is smart. (I wasn't *that* smart.) He'll win a scholarship."

I would be the first member of our immediate family to attend college, she said.

I applied for financial aid. I applied for early admission at my university of choice.

The year went by. No word about a scholarship.

In the winter, I received a letter from the university; I was admitted, but there was no word about a scholarship. The economic pressure on my folks mounted.

Grandma's health began to fail.

Goldie Finkelstein was about ninety. She went from our house to a nursing home to a hospital. Mom now had two worries—her mother's health and her son's collegiate future.

Finally, Grandma went into a coma.

On a Friday morning in April, she died.

The next day an official-looking letter came. I had won a full scholarship.

—*Steve Lipman*

S*olomon* Schwartz* felt blessed. His was one of the happy marriages. He knew that many of his friends suffered bitterness and disappointment in their less-than-perfect unions, and that they led lives of quiet desperation. But he and his wife Minnie were truly soul mates. They loved each other deeply, shared the same values and ideals, and enjoyed an unusual camaraderie. Only one thing was missing from their life together to make it complete, and that was God's gift of children—but the Schwartzes were sure that the delay was only temporary.

Year after year, they waited expectantly, for the legion of doctors they consulted had found nothing wrong and assured them that they would indeed conceive. But the time arrived when Minnie could barely look at a baby carriage being pushed down the street by a beaming mother without a tear dimming her eye, and a lump would form in her throat whenever she heard the unmistakable wail of a newborn babe. In the past, she used to linger in front of infants-wear shops, caressing with her eyes the ruffles and bibs and embroidered lace; but now when she passed one, she simply quickened her pace and looked straight ahead.

It was in the twelfth year of their marriage that the elderly patriarch of the Schwartz family summoned Solomon into his study for an unexpected conference one day. "You know," the well-meaning but misinformed uncle said, "one of the most important *mitzvot* (commandments) in the Torah is *pru urevu*—be fruitful and multiply. Bringing children into this world is not only pleasurable, it is an obligation. We are responsible for perpetuating the species, for perpetuating the Jewish people. If your wife is barren for more than ten years, the Torah decrees, you must divorce her."

"No!" shouted Solomon in disbelief.

"It is the law," the uncle stated firmly.

"It's not possible that the Torah would want to dissolve a loving marriage—children or not!"

"Ask your rabbi if you don't believe me . . . anyway, I've already taken the liberty of speaking with Minnie and explaining the situation to her, and she is a woman of valor indeed. She has agreed not to stand in the way of your happiness and fulfilling the commandments; she does not want to deprive you of the possibility of having children with another woman. So she will give you a divorce without any contest or problem. She loves you and wants the best for you."

"Who are you to decide what is best for me?" Solomon hissed in fury. "My wife Minnie whom I love and adore and worship . . . she is the best thing for me; she is my entire world. I will not divorce her. I don't believe that any such law even exists. You're probably making the whole thing up!"

But later, when Solomon conferred with an

acquaintance who was an ordained rabbi, the friend shifted uneasily in his chair.

"There *is* such a law," he confessed to Solomon. "And in a different era, people did comply with its ruling. But today the rabbis are more lax in their interpretation of this law, and most do not advise divorce. And in your case, where you and Minnie have such a beautiful relationship and special love, there would be few clergymen, I am sure, who would urge you to consider that drastic course. Just forget that the conversation with your uncle ever happened and go on with your lives."

But things had been set in motion that could not be undone; things had spun out of control. Once persuaded to be the cause of martyrdom for the sake of her husband and future generations of Schwartzes, Minnie would not allow herself to be deterred. She was now committed wholeheartedly to the path of divorce.

"I was being selfish all these years," she cried. "It is usually the woman who is the infertile one. With another wife, you have a chance to have many children. I cannot stand in your way; I love you too much to deprive you."

And as much as Solomon argued, protested, and reasoned, Minnie remained stoic and steadfast. Her greatest sacrifice . . . her ultimate act of love . . . would be the relinquishment of her beloved husband to another.

When he handed her the *get* (Jewish writ of divorce), Solomon keened with grief. "Love you always," he said, brokenhearted.

"Eternally," she answered, aching.

Two weeks later, she called him on the phone and told him that she was pregnant.

"We'll get remarried right away!" he shouted. "I'm sure it's permissible. I'll call my uncle to ask how to proceed."

But the patriarch was unaccountably silent when Solomon jubilantly conveyed the momentous news.

"Well . . . yes . . . in normal cases, a couple can remarry," the patriarch said slowly. "But . . . this is not a normal case."

"What do you mean, this is not a normal case?" Solomon interrupted impatiently.

"Solomon, my child," the uncle sighed in commiseration, "you are a *kohen* (from the caste of high priests who served in the Temple). A *kohen* is subject to more rigorous rulings than the descendants of other tribes. . . . A *kohen*, I am very sorry to tell you, is not allowed to marry a divorced woman. And Minnie now falls into that category."

"But *I* divorced her, I, me, she was my wife . . ."

"Technically, it doesn't make a difference. She's still a divorced woman and you're still a *kohen*. I don't see how you can remarry her."

Solomon was stunned. Minnie, his greatest love, his most precious wife, was finally pregnant with their child, and he couldn't remarry her? It wasn't possible, was it?

But all the rabbinic scholars he consulted concurred with the patriarch's original ruling. He was a *kohen*, she was a divorcée, there was no way around it.

"But isn't there anything you can do?" he begged rabbi after rabbi. "A dispensation, an annulment, a nullification of some sort? Isn't there some technicality you can find to render the law to my advantage?"

There was no loophole, they answered sadly.

"Can't anyone anywhere do something?" he broke down in a rabbi's study one day.

The rabbi wanted to tell him with compassion that his quest was futile; that the greatest *tzaddik* (saint) in the world would be unable to help him; that no scholar anywhere who followed the *halacha* (Jewish law) would be able to find a way out for him — but he found himself saying these words instead:

"Why don't you seek the counsel of the Lubavitcher Rebbe?"

The Lubavitcher Rebbe was a celebrated sage headquartered in Crown Heights, Brooklyn. He had tens of thousands of disciples — followers and admirers throughout the world who fervently believed in the holy man's divinely inspired wisdom, intelligence, prescience, and healing powers. He had the ability, many said, to perform true miracles and to save lives.

For multitudes, he was the last chance, the last stop, the last court of appeal. He was all-encompassing in his love and unconditional acceptance of every Jew (regardless of affiliation) and often, secular Jews with the same travails as their more religious brethren would find themselves making pilgrimages to his famous address—770 Eastern Parkway—and coming away healed, the recipients of miracles.

Solomon Schwartz was observant enough to care about complying with the law, but he was not a Lubavitcher. He lived in California, and had never been personally touched by the Rebbe's charisma. Still, stories from the East Coast had flowed west, and he too had heard about the Rebbe's miracles. So, when the last rabbi he consulted blurted out: "How about trying the Lubavitcher Rebbe?" he felt it was worth a shot. He was told that the Rebbe opened his doors to the public on Sundays, and that petitioners received a brief audience on a first-come, first-served basis only.

A long line of supplicants waiting to see the Rebbe snaked around Eastern Parkway and spilled out onto its adjoining streets when Solomon arrived early Sunday morning. Hundreds of Jews of all stripes and persuasions streamed in rivulets toward the Rebbe's residence, hoping for their personal miracle. Solomon had caught the red-eye on Saturday night, but had not been able to sleep during the flight. Standing on this interminable line, he felt cranky and impatient. It would be hours before his turn with the Rebbe. But, he consoled himself, maybe it would be well worth the wait.

It wasn't. Five hours later, when his turn with the Rebbe finally came, Solomon whispered his heartbreaking tale and *halachic* conundrum into the Rebbe's listening ear. What he hoped for from the Rebbe renowned for his brilliance was either a groundbreaking, unprecedented piece of fancy *halachic* footwork that would release him from his deadlock, or at the very least, a heartfelt blessing. But neither of these was forthcoming. Instead the Rebbe simply studied Solomon for a fraction of a second, piercing his soul with burning intensity, and said: "Go talk to your mother."

"Wh-what?" stammered Solomon in frustration and despair.

"Go talk to your mother," the Rebbe said again.

Solomon's fuse blew. "I traveled three thousand miles for you to tell me to talk to my mother?" he railed in disbelief. "That's all you have to tell me?"

"Go talk to your mother," the Rebbe repeated a third time, and then waved him away.

Solomon walked the streets of Crown Heights, a lonely forlorn figure. He felt cheated, betrayed. The venerable sage was no holy man, after all. He was a charlatan, a hoaxer, a fraud! *Go talk to your mother.* What kind of advice was that?

Still . . . he stopped in his tracks to reconsider. It was interesting how the Rebbe seemed to know with certainty that he *had* a mother, that she was still alive. This knowledge could not be presumed of the average middle-aged man. And how *did* the Rebbe seem to know that he hadn't spoken to his mother in a very long time?

Over the years, he and his mother had sadly become estranged. They had had several disputes that had worn the threads of their relationship thin, and the mending that should have taken place had just never occurred. It had been months since they had last spoken, and she wasn't even aware of the momentous events that had recently taken place in his life: the divorce, Minnie's miraculous pregnancy, his frantic search for a *halachic* way to remarry her.

Go talk to your mother, the Rebbe had said.

He didn't know what the Rebbe meant by this cryptic remark, but maybe it was time for him to see his mother, anyway.

Her face crumpled when she opened the door, and she pulled him to herself in a long embrace.

"It's been too long," she cried. "Over *narishkeit* (silliness). Come into the kitchen, I have fresh coffee and I just made cheese Danish, still hot from the oven. Where's Minnie?"

He told her everything.

About the patriarch's meddling; Minnie's insistence on a divorce to free him to have children with someone else; the sudden, joyful upheaval caused by her unexpected pregnancy; his search for a *halachic* recourse. . . .

"So, Mom," he ended his litany, "can you imagine such a problem?"

"Son," his mother said slowly and deliberately, staring intently into his face. "There *is* no problem. . . . I never could bring myself to tell you before, but obviously now I must. It is true that your father was a *kohen,* so naturally you assumed that you are one, too, since it's passed down through the male line. But you're not a *kohen* at all, and so you're free to remarry Minnie. . . . Son, the Rebbe was right when he told you to talk to me. You see . . . you're adopted."

*F*or the last half-year of her too short life, twenty-three-month-old Marlee Kalman had consistently played with one particular toy that was, for her, a seeming source of endless fascination and enchantment. It constantly absorbed her attention and its novelty—despite so much time—never wore off. It was a musical teapot, white with pink flowers, and a popular nursery song issued from its fuchsia lid whenever a switch was turned on.

Marlee's mother, Pam Kalman, loved to observe her little girl inspect the teapot with such intense concentration, turning it around and over and upside down, tirelessly attempting to locate the origins of its music. If it had belonged to her daughter, Pam would have unhesitatingly described it as being Marlee's most prized possession.

But Marlee was *not* in fact the proud owner of the musical teapot, despite her proprietary attitude toward it. The plaything she adored more than anything else in the world actually belonged to Rebecca, the daughter of Pam's best friend, Marci.

"I wish I could find another teapot like this one for Marlee," Marci would often murmur to Pam, whenever she came to visit. The two had been best friends for twelve years, and spent several days a week together in one another's homes. The musical teapot had been a gift for Rebecca from a relative who lived abroad, and nothing like it seemed to be available in the Chicago area where they resided. A devoted friend, Marci had scoured the neighborhood stores persistently, but had been unable to unearth a similar one anywhere. So she had bought Marlee a tea party set instead, but it was the music that seemed to entrance the toddler, not the teapot itself.

"You know, Pam," Marci would frequently repeat, "if I had been the one to buy the teapot myself, I would gladly offer it to Marlee. But since it was a gift from a relative, I don't feel right about giving it away."

"Of course you can't do that . . ." Pam would protest. "Goodness knows, we're here often enough that Marlee gets more than her fair chances to play with the teapot. Anyway, I'm sure she'll soon tire of it."

But she never did.

Each time they entered Marci's home, Marlee would make an immediate beeline for the teapot, clutch it possessively, walk around the room with it tucked under her arm, and then sit down and play with it for about an hour at a time. Engrossed in animated conversation while Marlee played, the two mothers' gazes would flicker occasionally toward the girl, and then they would break off their tete-a-tete to comment:

". . . It's amazing how she never tires of that toy, Pam."

"I think she's trying to figure out how an inanimate object can play music!"

"But that kind of intense concentration is very unusual

for a child that age."

"Hey, she's an unusual kid," Pam would laugh.

And then the two would resume their discussion, laughing, chatting, content with their lives as young mothers, happily planning for their childrens' future, never knowing that there was no future for Marlee, who would soon be cut down in her prime, her light snuffed out in one horrible moment that would last for eternity.

It was the screeching of brakes and an inhuman wail from the anguished driver that heralded the end.

Marlee, too small to be seen from the rear view window of a car as it backed up, had been struck down in the driveway of her own home.

She was carried into the Kalman home, where Pam frantically performed CPR and mouth-to-mouth. When the paramedics arrived, they worked on Marlee's lifeless form for half an hour but refusing to give up, rushed her to the Trauma Center where doctors continued their herculean efforts.

The attempts were valiant and untiring, but they were fruitless. Marlee had never really had a chance to be revived; her death had been sudden and swift.

The team of doctors who filed into the waiting room to tell the Kalmans seized upon that fact as some small consolation.

"It happened so fast she didn't feel any pain," they proffered as comfort.

"How can you be so sure?" Pam demanded,

desperately wanting to believe them.

Marci, who had rushed to the hospital with her husband Steven to be with the Kalmans, touched Pam's shoulder compassionately.

"All I want to know is that Marlee is okay," Pam sobbed in anguish.

"She's okay . . . she's okay . . . I promise you she's okay," Marci murmured gently, folding Pam into her embrace.

Throughout the ordeal, Marci never strayed from Pam's side, a pillar of strength and fortitude. But after the papers had been signed and the funeral parlor notified, Pam turned to her friend and made the request: "Marci, I can't go home and see the pool of blood on the driveway and the pool of blood on the living room floor. Could you go clean it up for me?"

When Marci and her husband Steven finally returned to their own home later that night, drained from the last ordeal of mopping up Marlee's blood, they staggered up the steps to their front door, bone-weary and in a state of shell-shock. As Marci fumbled for the keys, Steven said: "It was good of your mother to take Rebecca for the night. I don't think I could handle . . ." He paused and said slowly, "She *did* take Rebecca, didn't she, Marci?"

Marci looked at him, surprised.

"Yes, of course, Mom took Rebecca, I told you that, didn't I?"

"What's the matter?" she asked as a look of consternation crossed his face.

"Well, if Rebecca is at your mother's, and there's no babysitter here, and no one's home, *who* is making that sound?"

"What sound?" Marci asked confused, as Steven flung open the front door and rushed into the center hall.

She heard his sharp intake of breath as he headed into the living room, off to the left of the center hall.

"Oh, my God," she heard him say.

On the floor of the living room, which had been converted into a playroom, the musical teapot was playing its familiar song.

"I guess you left it on this morning and forgot about it," Steven said as he bent down to pick up the teapot and shut it off.

"But Rebecca didn't play with the teapot today . . ." Marci said slowly. "And Marlee wasn't here this morning, either. I don't understand . . ."

"This is weird!" Steven interrupted her. "The switch is in the *off* position."

"What do you mean the switch isn't *on*? How can it be playing the music, if the switch isn't on?"

"Come see for yourself . . ." Steven showed Marci that the switch was pulled to the off position. "Maybe there's some kind of a short . . ." he muttered, and began fiddling with the off and on switch, moving the lever back and forth.

But the music continued to pour out of the teapot, unabated. All of Steven's maneuverings couldn't get it to stop.

"This is giving me the goosebumps," Marci shouted. "If you can't get the switch lever fixed, just pull out the batteries."

The batteries dropped into Steven's hand as he forced them out, but still the music played.

The two looked at each other, numb with shock.

"How can the music be playing from the teapot, *when there are no batteries inside?*" Marci screamed.

Steven grabbed the wires in the battery box, and yanked those out too.

The teapot continued to play its song.

"Do you believe this?" Steven muttered, staring with disbelief at the teapot.

"Get it out of here!" Marci cried, "get rid of it!"

Steven hurled the teapot down the basement stairs.

And as it hit the bottom of the stairs with a thud, its musical refrain wafted up to the first floor where Marci and Steven stood, stunned and pale-faced.

All night long, the music never ceased, and finally, Marci picked up the phone and called Pam.

Pam could barely recognize Marci's voice; she was hyperventilating, weeping, and gulping—all at the same time.

"Pam!" Marci sobbed. "I don't want to upset you, but I have to tell you this. Marlee is *here* playing at my house tonight . . . I think she wants me to give you a message . . ."

The fog that had engulfed Pam from the outset of the accident lifted a little.

"All I had prayed for in the hospital was some sign, some assurance that Marlee was okay," she says today, almost five years after the terrible tragedy of December 23, 1995. "When Marci called me with the news, I knew that the sign I had prayed for had appeared. Marlee had let me know that wherever she was, she was fine . . ."

The day of Marlee's funeral, Marci tiptoed to her cellar door and opened it tentatively. Drifting up the stairs, was the unmistakable music of the teapot, playing ceaselessly, endlessly, for all eternity, Marlee's song.

Without batteries and without wires, the teapot had remained undeterred. Marlee's song played on.

—*Pam Kalman*

*M*y father and mother were great aficionados of classical music, and my father was especially enthralled by the violin. It was his greatest wish that I learn to play this instrument.

When I was still very young, I began studying the violin with a renowned member of the Hamburg Symphony Orchestra, who told my parents that I possessed some talent. My father decided that serious study required a better violin than the one I was currently using, and he presented me with a very fine, very expensive instrument of superior vintage. The day he gave me the violin was one of the high points of my childhood: He glowed with pride and I with the excitement of a budding musician. It was a day I would long remember. I was seven years old.

In 1938, the halcyon days we had enjoyed as German Jews living in Hamburg came to an abrupt end. One Sabbath afternoon, I returned home from synagogue to find two officers of the Gestapo sitting in my living room, waiting for my father. They had told my mother that he was required for a few hours to fill out some forms at the local police station. Although he too was on his way home from synagogue, where he had tarried after services, my mother loudly and insistently told them that he was away in Berlin. She was, of course, well intentioned as she made her vocal protestations, only wanting to shield her husband from trouble. How could she have known that, growing impatient, the Nazis would take me instead?

I was seventeen years old that Shabbat afternoon when the Nazis hauled me away—ostensibly to the police station, but transported instead to one of the first concentration camps erected outside Hamburg. Everything happened very quickly, and I was not given the opportunity to apprise my parents of my whereabouts. I could only envision how devastated they must have been when I failed to return home, and then disappeared completely from their lives.

For the next seven years, I was shipped from one camp to another, including Sachsenhausen, Auschwitz, Buna, and finally Bergen-Belsen, where I was liberated on April 15, 1945. Few people were interned in concentration camps for such a length of time, and fewer yet survived.

After several months in a DP (displaced persons) camp, I told the authorities that I wanted to return to Hamburg to search for my family. A few other male refugees from the camp whom I had befriended decided to accompany me, since they were without families and had already sadly discovered that their hometowns were *Judenrein* (cleansed of all Jews). Homeless and rootless, they had nowhere to go and nowhere to be, so they decided to join me on my own personal pilgrimage.

As we entered the outskirts of Hamburg on a small

bus that the British had loaned us, my eyes widened in shock to see the city almost exactly as I had left it. There was no rubble; there were no bombed-out buildings; there was no lunar landscape of destruction. All the buildings were standing upright and intact, untouched, unchanged, as if the war had never happened. Hamburg, I had been sure, would be desolate and bleak. I began to cry bitterly.

One of my friends touched my shoulder compassionately. "Why are you crying so hard?" he asked tenderly. "Because it means so much for you to see that the city was not annihilated?"

"No," I said. "I am crying *because* this city was not annihilated. It would have made me happier to see it in ruins."

It was the Jewish community that had been ravaged instead. Demolished, eradicated, gone. Almost no one was left, including my parents and siblings. But I was able to learn their fate from the few Jews who had miraculously survived and remained in Hamburg. My sisters, I was told, left for America the day after I disappeared. My father smuggled himself into Belgium the day after that. But my mother, my dear, sweet, precious mother who herself had several visas in her name and could easily have joined my sisters on the ship to New York, refused to leave.

"How can I leave here without Leo?" she had objected strenuously. "We don't know where he is . . .

but hopefully, he'll come back soon. And how will he feel if we are all gone, and his home is empty? Where will he go, what will he do? . . . And another thing," she added, "If I stay here, I can try to find out what happened to him. I can keep on going to the police station and other offices. I can look for him; I can work for his release. In America, I will be too far away to be able to accomplish anything. No, I can't leave; I must stay here and wait for my son."

In her heart, it seemed that my mother believed that I *would* return. Over the next few years, she had many opportunities to escape, but she passed them all up. She was waiting for me to come back home.

But when I finally did, she herself was gone. She had been rounded up, together with the last remaining Jewish women of Hamburg, in April 1941, and shipped to a concentration camp, where she became reduced to a statistic — the Six Million.

Despite the horror of my personal discoveries, I still remained for a while in Hamburg. Like my friends, I too was now homeless; where could I go? Two weeks later, a man stood on the threshold of the apartment where I was temporarily living and rang the bell.

"Is it really you, Leo?" he asked. "I am so overjoyed to see you! I could not believe it when people told me that you were alive. . . . Everyone's talking . . . *Weissman's back, Weissman's survived!*"

He noticed my blank expression. "Oh, you don't re-cognize me, Leo? It's Franz Schneider* . . . remember me?"

Franz Schneider! His face was not familiar, but his story was unforgettable. In the tense prewar years, everyone in the Jewish community had talked about this man and knew his remarkable saga well.

Franz Schneider had been born and raised a Christian, and he was a churchgoing man. In 1936, however, he suddenly approached the rabbi of our synagogue and told him he wanted to convert to Judaism. The rabbi was dumbfounded. The atmosphere in Hamburg was already permeated with the malignant hatred that bred the inevitable, and the growing anti-Jewish legislation and economic sanctions were already in evidence. Judaism in general discourages proselytizing, but 1936 was certainly the most incongruous time to contemplate a conversion.

"Why would you want to do such a thing at such a time?" the rabbi asked, incredulous at the bizarre request. "Don't you know how much we are hated? How tenuous our fate is?"

"My dear Rabbi," Schneider replied resolutely. "It is precisely *because* of the horrible atmosphere now and the terrible things that are happening that I wish to convert. I cannot bear to stand by and witness the pain of my Jewish brothers, the discrimination, the injustices, the outrages to which they are subjected. I want to display my solidarity with my Jewish brethren and know what it's like to feel their pain, and that is why I want to convert now."

The rabbi flatly refused Schneider's request, and his congregants threw their support behind his action. But Schneider was determined, and had in fact already started studying for his conversion long before he made his intentions clear. He would not be swayed from his purpose—not by the rabbi, nor by the congregants, nor by his own family. Despite intense pressure exerted on him by all of the above, Schneider ultimately had his way and underwent a conversion.

If he failed at discouraging the conversion, the rabbi had at least been successful in persuading Schneider to keep his new identity secret. "In these precarious times," the rabbi told him, "you will be much more helpful to the Jewish community as a Christian than as a Jew. Let us hope this horrible period will end soon. But in the meantime, if you don't tell anyone about the conversion, you can serve as our conduit to the outside world."

And that is precisely what happened. As the stranglehold on Hamburg Jewry tightened, Frank Schneider became a lifeline for the last remaining Jews. As an official "Christian," he had access to money, food, medicine, and other critical items unavailable to the Jews, and he supplied the remnants of the Jewish community with these items. Single-handedly, Franz Schneider kept Hamburg's Jews alive until one by one, they were rounded up and taken away. A Christian to the outside world, Schneider survived.

This was the same Franz Schneider who now stood

at my door. As soon as he uttered his name, memories came flooding back. How could I forget him? His courage and compassion had been legendary; his humanity filled us with awe.

I welcomed Schneider into my apartment, and it was only when he had crossed into my modest rooms that I noticed he had an object cradled under his arm.

"Your beloved mother," he began, "who loved you so much, waited for news of you every day and longed for your return. She never gave up; she always believed that you would come back home. But one morning . . . perhaps she had a premonition that her own days were numbered . . . she approached me with an unusual request.

"'My dear Schneider,'" she said, "'of all the prized possessions that my son Leo held dear, I know it was his violin that he cherished more than anything else. So, I want to ask you a tremendous favor. You, as a so-called Christian, will surely survive this war. Can you keep his violin, safeguard it for him? I believe that Leo will survive and come back home. Can you hold it for him until he does? Perhaps it will give him comfort and remind him of the happy times we had together as a family, and how much we loved him.'"

"I wanted to protest what your mother left unspoken: her conviction that she would not be able to give the violin to you herself. But I could not force empty platitudes and offend her with false cheer. I nodded silently, she handed me the violin, and then she was gone. A few days later, she was rounded up with the last of the remaining Jews and never seen again."

Franz Schneider withdrew the object cradled under his arm and I reached for my old violin. A torrent of memories came rushing up at me: I remembered the day when my father had first given it to me, as my mother beamed with pride. I also remembered the little concerts I performed for them as I grew more proficient, and the sense of normalcy then that I would never know again. My mother had been right: Of everything I owned, the violin held the greatest sentimental value for me, recalling a time in my life that could never be resurrected.

Today, I am eighty years old and my eyesight is fading fast. I can't read the notes anymore, and even if I did play the violin, my hands would tremble. But despite these things, it gives me great comfort to know that my violin is here with me, in my home in Florida, a testament to my mother's unflagging devotion and Schneider's great strength of character. They are both gone now, but the violin remains, and with it their legacy of love.

—*Leo Weissman*

S_{mall} talk. Chitchat. Tense silences. Awkward pauses.

First dates, especially "blind" ones, are often filled with uneasy moments as nervous singles shift uncomfortably in their seats and strain to make bright, animated chatter.

But Shelly Brown* and Rob Shapiro* had overcome that hurdle easily. As Rob escorted Shelly out of the high-rise building she lived in on the Upper West Side of Manhattan, they stumbled over a homeless man sprawled across the sidewalk in a drunken stupor. Both bent over the man in compassion, trying to rouse him, and then they called the police. By the time the brouhaha had subsided, the ice between the two had been broken.

Afterwards, as they walked along Broadway toward their destination, they had much to discuss. Both commented on the sorry plight of vagrants in New York City, and Rob confided that once a month he volunteered at a shelter for the homeless. Shelly arched her eyebrows in surprise. Once a month *she* volunteered at a soup kitchen. The conversation took off from there, as both social activists discussed urban blight, social ills, and local politics. Nary a word was spoken about their own personal histories.

But as soon as they made the transition from the dark city streets to the brightly lit restaurant where they had reservations, the conversation trailed off.

It was then that Rob made his foray into the usual first-date concrete-data here's-my-resume chatter:

"So," he said, turning to her brightly, "you know . . . it's a funny thing—but my ex-wife is also named Shelly."

"Is that so?" she smiled. "I didn't want to tell you this, but guess what? *My* ex-husband is also a Rob!"

"Hah," he laughed, "that's cute. Well, I guess there are a lot of Robs around, right? Popular soap opera name at the time I was born."

"So . . . I understand you have a few children. Why don't you tell me about them?" Shelly prompted.

"Well, there's Miriam, age three, Daniel, age five, and Joey, age ten," he said proudly. "Is anything wrong?" he asked quickly, as he saw her face turn pale.

"Well, I don't know how to tell you this . . ." she said. "Do you want to know about *my* children?"

"Sure, go ahead."

"Well, there's Miriam, age three . . . Daniel, age five . . . and Joey, age ten!"

His jaw dropped. "You're kidding, right?" he asked, weakly.

"I know, this is downright weird . . . but it's true."

They both fell silent.

"Hey, you know," Rob offered, laboring to fill in the widening gap in conversation, "my ex-wife is getting married next week . . ."

"Oh, no!" Shelly jumped from her seat. "Tell me this is a joke."

"What's the matter?" Rob asked, perplexed.

"My ex-husband is getting married next week, too! . . . and he's marrying somebody named . . . Shelly!"

"Wait a second . . . your ex-husband's last name isn't by any chance Rosenberg, is it?"

"And your ex-wife's last name isn't Simmons, is it?" Shelly asked.

"What do *you* think?" Rob grinned back.

So Shelly and Rob, who had been married to Shelly and Rob, united in holy matrimony, just like . . . Shelly and Rob.

And since both had custody of their children, their lively household now consisted of two Miriams, age three, two Daniels, age five, and two Joeys, age ten. Who ever said that *opposites* attract?

I was never my mother's daughter; it was my father's imprint instead that was clearly stamped on me. Our faces, people exclaimed, were almost identical; our eyes the same smoky hazel color; our physiques (my one true regret) hewn from similar stone. But beyond physical appearance, our spirits seemed uncommonly linked; there was such an intense connection between us that sometimes I thought we had to be twin souls.

When my father died, I was thirty-three, married, and a mother, but the impact of his death was apocalyptic nonetheless, despite the three bulwarks of maturity, marital status, and motherhood.

"So how old was he?" insensitive people would ask, as if the age of one's deceased parent really mattered (the intimation being: It's okay to grieve if he was cut down in his prime, but if he was elderly, authorization to mourn extensively is denied).

As it happened, he was only sixty-two and, yes, far too young to leave this world.

One of the wisest, most beautiful, and most comforting customs in the Jewish tradition is the *shiva*: the seven days of official mourning during which the bereaved are given a context, parameters, and—most important—permission to grieve. During this time, the family is sequestered in the house and well-wishers visit to extend their sympathy and offer consolation.

On the third or fourth day of the *shiva*, there was an interlude between visitors and I retreated to the kitchen for some quiet contemplation. It was then that I first noticed the stack of papers, written in my father's familiar and beloved spidery handwriting, heaped up in a careless pile on the kitchen table. I began to sift through the pile, fingers trembling. Only a few days before, I wouldn't have given the stack a second thought, but now the papers had become transmogrified into precious relics. They had assumed a new significance by virtue of the fact that my beloved father had touched them with his callused hands. There were his signature doodles scrawled in the margins of the notepaper, the coffee stains that discolored its edges. Only a few short days ago, my father had been vitally alive. Now he was gone, and, ironically, what remained behind to testify to his existence were inanimate objects and lifeless paraphernalia.

I sifted through the papers, searching for clues to his last days. What would they yield? What testament exactly was I hoping to find? Perhaps, like every other bereaved child (no matter what the age), I sought some sign that his vital life force had not been wiped out completely.

Most of the papers were inconsequential, and I laid them aside impatiently. But then I pulled out a page that made my hands freeze and my heart stop.

It was a poem in Yiddish that my father (a prolific Yiddish and Hebrew writer) had written just before he died—a poem that none of us had known about and that might never have been discovered had I not begun to examine the pile. My blood ran cold as I read the verses that so eloquently expressed the despair he had felt at the end of his life. In rough English translation, the poem read:

> *The telephone stands mutely*
> *Desperately wishing to ring*
> *Hoping that news of the outside world it can bring*
> *To the one who waits for a friendly voice*
> *But the phone can't ring, it has no choice*
> *No one is dialing its number to say hello*
> *Where are all the people I used to know?*
> *Everyone has forgotten me, the lines don't hum*
> *The phone is forlorn, and rebuked, it stands dumb.*

As I read the poem, my heart ached for my father, who had apparently felt so alone during the last days of his life. And I only wished he could have known how mistaken he was about his place in society—how all the pews in the funeral parlor had been filled to overflowing with people who loved and admired him; how many sympathy letters, phone calls, baskets, and bouquets had poured into the house to convey anguish at his death.

I though of the irony inherent in my father's last words: now the phone didn't stop ringing with calls of sympathy from those who had loved him and would miss him forever. And suddenly, as if a spell had been cast over me, I moved from my chair in the kitchen to my bedroom, where I began to write a poem myself. My father's poem had been called "The Silent Phone." Mine in turn was entitled "The Busy Telephone: A Response."

> *Oh, Father, the phone doesn't stop ringing*
> *As people call from everywhere, your praises singing*
> *Telling of your greatness, your talents commending*
> *With sighs from the heart and tears never-ending*
> *A tragedy, a shame that you never really felt*
> *The love and esteem in which you were held*
> *And I have to ask them: shouldn't these things have*
> *   been said long ago*
> *To the person who needed to hear them and still . . .*
> *   does not know?*
> *This is the irony of the human race: our sin that we wait*
> *We say the things we feel deeply only when it is far*
> *   too late.*

When I finished writing the poem, I shook myself out of a mental state that some would label a reverie and others might call "flow" but that I felt was more akin to a trance. Looking at the notebook in my lap, I shook my head in disbelief. I was not incredulous that I had written a poem (I have been writing poetry since I was eight years old); nor was I astonished that of all the times to write, I had incongruously penned one smack in the middle of *shiva*. No, it was neither of these things that caused me to gasp in wonderment at my own authorship: What made me tremble in fear was the fact that I, Yitta

Halberstam—whom everyone teased about her broken Yiddish; who barely knew how to write an elementary sentence in the language of her forebears—I had just written a piece in *flawless* literary Yiddish.

My parents had always spoken Yiddish to one another, but when I was a toddler growing up in Pittsburgh, I was confused by the dissonance of the two languages: Yiddish used exclusively at home, English in the rest of the world. When I turned two and a half and still could barely speak a few words in either language (how things have changed!), the pediatrician advised my mother to use English exclusively with me, since I appeared to be confused. Within a few short weeks, I was speaking complete sentences in English, but the pattern had already been established, and my parents were never able to revert back to speaking Yiddish to me.

Yet here I was now, at thirty-three, staring at the first poem that I had ever written in Yiddish, and, stranger still, it was . . . impeccable.

I blinked. I was mystified and frightened. How had this happened? I failed to understand it myself. When I showed it to my mother and siblings later that evening, they looked at me suspiciously. I wasn't capable of this kind of work in Yiddish—they knew that as well as I. Yet they had all seen me retreat to my bedroom alone and emerge with the poem. Clearly, no one had helped me—so where had the poem come from?

Two days later, I was once again ensconced in the

kitchen during an interval between visitors, and I began to survey the room with renewed interest. This was, after all, where my father had always worked. The homely kitchen, therefore, was now elevated in meaning and importance: It had become a shrine. So now I toured the ordinary kitchen with fresh eyes, and I saw something that had escaped my notice before. My father's lamp—an old-fashioned standing lamp that he used to illuminate his writing as he worked—had been pushed into a corner, and I imagined that it looked mournful. *What happens to a man's possessions once he's gone?* I wondered. *Do they too somehow feel the pain of his leave-taking?*

My mental state of two days before returned. I was transported once again to a different universe, under the influence of a heightened awareness that held me in its grip. As if in a trance, I rose once more, took paper and pen into the bedroom, and wrote a second poem—this one a paean to "The Standing Lamp." I wrote:

> *The standing lamp my father used is sitting* shiva *alone*
> *No one pays attention to his keening; no one hears*
>   *him groan.*
> *He doesn't understand where his friend has gone; the*
>   *man with whom he was so deeply bound*
> *The man with the words of fire: where can he now be*
>   *found?*
> *It was his brilliant light that helped the man create*

That was his mission in life, after all, to illuminate.
The partnership, however, has suddenly been broken
And of the two of them only the lamp is left, a lifeless
* token.*
His purpose in life is over to which he was born
And now he's pushed in a corner, forgotten and forlorn.
No one sees him, no one needs him, he is offended
Against his will, his life's calling has suddenly been
* ended.*
The lamp is extinguished; gone is its light.
The light of my father is extinguished
And now we are shrouded in endless night.

When I finished this second poem, I gazed at it in
even greater astonishment than I had felt when I had
written the first. For once again, it was written in a
highly literary Yiddish—a Yiddish I didn't know, a
Yiddish I didn't own. But if I hadn't written it, who had?

A week later, the *Algemeiner Journal,* a Yiddish weekly
where my father had worked as both editor and
columnist, published my two poems. Those people who
were not personal friends and did not know my linguistic
history congratulated me effusively and praised the
work. But those who knew me more intimately and had
heard me labor over the same language that was now
flawlessly printed in the paper accosted me skeptically
on the streets of Brooklyn.

The confrontation would run along these lines:
"Okay, Yitta, I've heard you speak Yiddish. And I know

you never wrote a single poem in Yiddish before. So tell me the truth . . . who wrote those poems?"

And having pondered this very same question myself during dark nights of longing for my beloved parent, I could only answer them with what I knew was the absolute truth: "My father."

The kabbala states that during the seven days of *shiva*, the soul of the departed hovers around the household, to watch family members in a last great burst of yearning and to try to ensure their welfare. The spirit is not yet in transition, and in mysterious ways is fully present with the family as they grieve.

At the end of the *shiva* period, it is customary among many Hasidic and Orthodox Jews to leave the house and walk around the block, escorting the departed soul out of the family's domain forever.

I never wrote a Yiddish poem *before* my father's death, and I never wrote one *after.* Having considered all the rational possibilities as to how words I barely knew and hardly recognized could possibly have been penned by me, I could only come up with one explanation that made sense: The poems had been authored by my father himself—his last great creative effort and his own inimitable way of bidding me farewell.

— *Yitta Halberstam*

*M*y mother has a gift for finding gold. And not just gold—other things, too. I remember walking with her as a small child and finding coins on the sidewalk, one after the other—not just pennies, but nickels, dimes, and quarters. There was the time her wallet was stolen in a large city. A few minutes later, a gust of wind blew a tightly folded $50 bill right into her face after someone else had lunged for it and missed. Then there was the slightly battered 14-karat-gold charm holder, with charms attached, that she found at a bus stop on a quiet rural road and sent to me at university ("Here—I'll never be able to track down the owner, and I don't wear charms," she wrote). Then there are the rare times Mom's bought a state lottery ticket and won the small prize—and shared it. But for me the following incident stands out the most.

One night when I was about ten years old, we were coming out of a local family restaurant. I noticed what seemed to me a glint of moonlight on a puddle. But my mother bent down and picked up a shining object that turned out to be a heavy gold bracelet, apparently made for a man. It had no identification.

"Wow, look at this!" exclaimed my mother, showing us her find. "It must be worth a lot of money. Okay, everyone, get in the car—we're going right to the police station." After the extra treat of a nighttime ride on the back-country roads, we arrived. The officer on duty took the bracelet, filled out the appropriate forms, and told Mom that if nobody claimed the bracelet after a certain amount of time—I think it was six months—it would become her legal property.

Sure enough, months later, the phone rang. "Ma'am, no one's claimed the bracelet. It's yours now, and you can come pick it up."

A few years later—I think I may have been at university then—my parents were leaving a local restaurant. My mother noticed something shiny on the ground and bent to pick it up. It was a gold bracelet, exactly the same style as the one she had found some years earlier, only smaller and slimmer—evidently made for a woman. "I think I found the 'hers' part of the 'his and hers' set," Mom said, as she headed back to the police station.

As before, no one came to claim the bracelet, and so my mother became the legal owner of a matching set!

—*Rahel Jaskow*

There are some people who find God everywhere, and who interpret familiar signs and commonplace omens as emblems of His presence in their everyday lives. Then there are those human beings to whom God appears in more unlikely places—individuals to whom He is revealed in singular ways not generally experienced by the public at large. Some of these people may tell you that it was a song on the radio that offered confirmation, comfort, or clear-cut advice at the precise moment they needed it; others will confess that it was a television commercial that proved uncannily prescient right after they turned a question over to the Universe.

Television doesn't talk to Beth Schwartz* of San Diego, California, nor to Shellie Shreiner of Hartford, Connecticut. The two women on opposite coasts don't even know each other, but what they do share is a common conviction that God speaks to them through . . . license plates.

"It was five o'clock in the morning," Beth remembers, "and I was driving up the freeway from San Diego to Los Angeles, on my way to a court appearance with my ex-husband. I was just three months pregnant with the first of the children that I was to have with my new husband, and I was extremely tense about the upcoming proceedings. The divorce had been extremely messy and mean, and I was bracing myself for more of the same. The results of that morning's court appearance would have major reverberations for my life. I longed for some harbinger, some sign that would indicate a positive outcome.

"As I sped down the highway, I could not help but notice an orange and black truck weaving in and out of traffic, alternately alongside me or just ahead. Its license plate startled me. SCHNEIDER, it read—the very name of the judge before whom I was about to appear that morning. *Did the license plate have any import?* I wondered, as the truck proceeded at a regular clip in front of me, then disappeared for a while into the flow of traffic, then reappeared once again. This happened about five or six times. I had been valiantly trying to get my mind off the imminent court battle, but the truck's license plate actually achieved the reverse effect.

"At 8:00 A.M. I found myself stuck in L.A. traffic, just ten blocks from the courthouse where I was scheduled to appear in half an hour. Traffic had come to a virtual standstill, and my anxiety mounted. I also felt deep-seated resentment toward my ex-spouse whom I had had to drag into court. It was *his* fault that I was not sleeping in my bed right now, curled up contentedly under the covers. It was *his* fault that I was pinned in on all sides by a maze of cars that left me feeling trapped and essentially helpless in a situation over which I had no control.

"Just then a car pulled up in front of me, flashing its unusual license plate: RDY 2 WIN. Despite the havoc around me, I had to smile and feel infused with newfound hope. So when I finally made it into the courtroom, my stride was confident and self-assured.

"The license plate proved prophetic and gave me a much-needed boost of positive energy: I did indeed win my court case that morning; all I had really needed was the extra push the appearance of those two license plates gave me.

"For both license plates—SCHNEIDER and RDY 2 WIN—had brought me hope and confirmation. They gave me the nudge I needed in order to fight a good fight and claim a victory that ultimately changed my life."

∾

Shellie has a similar story to recount.

"For days I had been feeling queasy and unwell. I couldn't quite pinpoint what was wrong with me; it didn't feel like the flu or a stomach virus, nor was it an ordinary garden-variety cold. But something was definitely not quite right. . . . *Had I picked up some strange illness from one of the preschoolers I teach every day?* I wondered.

"It was December 4, 1979, and I was on my way to the Jewish Community Center that houses my preschool class. It is my custom every morning to pray to God in the car, and He drives to work with me every single day.

"I was in the midst of having my usual chat with God that morning, when a certain suspicion suddenly struck me. 'Okay, God,' I said, 'if I'm pregnant, could you please have the fetus tap my stomach three times?' Then I laughed at my own irreverence and at the preposterousness of my proposal. 'Okay, God,' I hastily apologized, 'let me amend that. That is asking too much even from You. Could you just please send me a sign, any sign to let me know if I'm pregnant?'

"At that very moment, a red sports Mercedes pulled up in front of me—seemingly out of nowhere—flashing the license plate MOMMY.

"My mouth dropped open. God has always been very obliging, but this was what you call *fast work*.

"After school, I went to a lab for a blood test, and when the nurse told me that indeed, I was pregnant, she seemed disappointed—almost indignant—at my lack of surprise. Go explain that I've already been told by a Higher Source than her!

"In 1981, I was driving down a road in Connecticut, my by-then-toddler comfortably ensconced in her car seat in the back, when I had a sudden flashback to that momentous day two years before.

"I started reminiscing with my husband and wondered aloud: 'Maybe I was hallucinating or imagining the whole thing? Do you think I could have really seen the Mercedes with that license plate?'

"And at the very moment that I asked him this question, the exact same red Mercedes pulled out in front of me — seemingly out of nowhere — flashing its by-now familiar license plate: MOMMY.

"'Yup,' my husband laughed. 'I would say you really did see a car like that!"

Traditionally, Miami, Los Angeles, and New York are the three cities in the United States to which most Israelis flock — both as tourists and as immigrants. Pittsburgh, Pennsylvania, on the other hand, has never proven to be a major magnet for the expatriates, and Hebrew is certainly not the lingua franca of the grass-roots natives there. So Eric Blaustein perked up his ears attentively on Rosh Hashanah night last September when he heard an uncommon language — Hebrew — being spoken on the street outside his temple in Mount Lebanon, a suburb of Pittsburgh. People often laugh about how much Hebrew is spoken in New York, but certainly no one has ever made that claim about Pittsburgh. Nostalgic to hear the language that he once knew well, Eric Blaustein listened appreciatively, and then, unable to suppress his curiosity, approached the Hebrew-speaking group. Who were they, he wanted to know, and what were they doing in — of all places — Pittsburgh?

"My company just transferred me," a young man in the group explained. "And of course my family has relocated with me," he said, introducing his wife and children. He then gestured toward an older man and woman at his side. "These are my parents. They don't live here, but they came to visit us for the High Holidays."

Eric felt drawn to the father, a man close to his age,

and began a halting conversation with him in his own rusty Hebrew. The older man was visibly impressed, even though Eric wasn't very fluent.

"Where'd you learn to speak Hebrew?" the Israeli asked, pleasantly surprised.

"I'm a survivor of the concentration camps," the German-born Blaustein replied. "I went to Israel after the war, and in 1948 I fought as a volunteer soldier during Israel's war of independence. I served with the Twelfth Brigade, Seventh Regiment."

The Israeli looked at Blaustein with quickened interest. "I know this is a long shot, but were you by any chance in the second company?"

Indeed, Blaustein said, he was.

A variety of emotions, which Eric couldn't quite decipher, danced across the Israeli's face. "You weren't in the third platoon, were you?"

Right again.

Then the Israeli asked a startling question: "Were you a second lieutenant?"

"Yes, as a matter of fact," Blaustein answered in amazement, "I *was* a second lieutenant."

"And your unit had only one second lieutenant, right?" the Israeli pressed on.

"Now, how would you know that?" Blaustein demanded, flustered by where the line of questioning was leading. "How could you *possibly* know that?"

"Because I've been looking for you for fifty-two

years!" the Israeli shouted, grabbing Eric's hand and pumping it vigorously. "Remember the French Commandos? You *saved my life!*"

It had happened fifty-two years ago, but the memory was as vivid as if it had been yesterday. In a flashback, Eric Blaustein remembered it all: The Negev . . . the Israeli advance unit made up of French volunteers under enemy attack by the Egyptians and almost out of ammunition . . . his own platoon being called on to rescue the stranded soldiers caught in the line of fire. Eric's unit had broken through enemy lines to pick up the dead and injured and bring them back to safety. And then there had been the one wounded soldier whom Eric had carried on his back . . . all the way to the field dressing station. Eric had made sure the soldier was tended to, and had then left, never learning the man's name nor his fate. But Eric was not easily forgotten by the man, who had been conscious throughout the ordeal and had stared at Eric's second lieutenant shoulder insignia, burning them into his memory.

All his life he had wanted to meet the man who had rescued him, so he could thank him.

"To think I had to come to Pittsburgh to meet you again!" the Israeli exclaimed, and went on to say that this was his first time here.

Eric Blaustein stared at him, incredulous. "But I wasn't even supposed to be here tonight," he told the man. "Every Rosh Hashanah my wife and I travel to

Chicago to be with our daughter, whose husband is a rabbi and who obviously can't leave his pulpit at this time. It's practically a tradition—we've done it for several years straight."

But this year he and his wife had suddenly decided to stay home in Mount Lebanon, for the first time since their daughter had moved to Chicago.

"The Israeli wound up coming to Pittsburgh for the first time, and I wound up staying for the first time," Eric told the *Pittsburgh Post*, "and we both wound up in the same synagogue together."

Both men felt that they had been touched by a miracle. The Israeli was thrilled that he was finally able to thank his benefactor, and Blaustein was touched to witness the miracle of life he had given this man, his son, and his grandchildren. Three generations stood before him now, testifying to the impact of his one action fifty-two years before.

It was a great way to start the New Year, both said.
—*Eric Blaustein*

They were fleeing the Nazis through the forests of Dej (in Transylvania) when their Hungarian guide, whom they had paid lavishly, disappeared. The Paneths—one of the most noble and distinguished Hasidic families in prewar Europe—had depended on the man to lead them to the border of Rumania. The guide had insisted that they put as much distance as possible between themselves and the city of Dej. Once their beloved hometown, now it had become a place of peril, reeking of danger and death.

The guide had left them encamped during the day, promising to return by nightfall. But when twenty-four hours had passed with no sign of the guide, they knew they were on their own. Now Grand Rabbi Paneth, his wife, and their eight children stumbled blindly through the forest, recognizing that the only One they could always depend upon was the Almighty above.

They walked at night and hid and rested by day, when discovery was more likely. Tired, weak, and hungry, they walked relentlessly, in search of food and shelter. Finally, they reached the edge of the forest where a little silo stood, seemingly unused and abandoned. They slipped inside and concealed themselves in the hayloft. At last they had some semblance of shelter, but they were all faint from hunger. None of them had eaten for forty-eight hours.

"We must go out and try to find some food," Mrs. Paneth told her husband resolutely. "We must take the risk of being found out. What difference does it make what a person dies of? Which is worse, to die of a gunshot or hunger?"

So she and her son Moishe left the barn and walked across a field where two laborers were tilling the soil. Having discarded their Hasidic attire in favor of the less conspicuous peasant garb, they hoped that their disguise would prove effective. Trying to pass as authentic peasants, they walked at a deliberately slow and casual pace. Mrs. Paneth's eyes studied the peasants, resting on one tall, neatly dressed man who seemed to stand out. She approached him boldly and asked: "Do you have God in your heart?"

The man flinched for a moment and then surveyed her and Moishe silently, as if assessing their situation.

"Oh good woman, what are you doing here?" he asked, instantly grasping their predicament. "Don't worry," he added quickly, "I won't give you away."

"My children are suffering so much," she cried. "They haven't eaten in two days. Can you help us?"

"Where are you hiding?" he asked. "I'll send my wife home to fill a basket with food."

"Don't worry," he reassured them again. "My name is Tarnowan and I'm the village minister and judge. I won't turn you in."

The two returned to the barn and told the others

about the encounter in the field. "He said he'll bring food as soon as he can. I think he can be trusted," Mrs. Paneth said.

True to his word, Tarnowan soon appeared at the barn, accompanied by his wife and baskets of food. On their arrival, Rabbi Paneth jumped to his feet. "I cannot begin to tell you how grateful I am to you for your kindness," he murmured. "You are saving our lives with this food." He extended his hand in greeting. "Thank you so much. I understand your are Judge Tarnowan. And my name is Yosef Paneth."

Tarnowan suddenly blanched, gazing at the Rabbi in awe and disbelief. "Paneth?" he asked in stupefaction. "You did say . . . Paneth?"

The rabbi was puzzled by Tarnowan's strange reaction.

"May I ask what your *father's* name was?" Tarnowan pressed on.

"Rabbi Yecheskel Paneth."

Now Tarnowan was white as a sheet, staring at the rabbi in open-mouthed wonder. "If it is true what you say—that you are indeed the son of Rabbi Yecheskel Paneth—then I owe you a good deed. Your father once performed a great favor for me, and now I can return it."

Trembling, the judge recounted the following story:

"Twenty years ago, when I was a police officer, my two-year-old son became deathly ill. My wife and I traveled all over the country, searching for a cure, but every single healer that we consulted was pessimistic and gave us a bleak prognosis. There was nothing to be done, they advised, the end was near. We tried hard not to be swayed by their negative words. We were not ready to give up on our son. Then I heard about a very holy rabbi who lived in the city of Dej. Being a religious person myself, I had no qualms about approaching a rabbi for a blessing for my son.

"When I arrived in the city, people directed me to a large building with many students milling about. I approached one young man and asked him if the great rabbi could give my son a blessing. He told me that he would go inside and see what he could do. A few minutes later, he returned saying that he had a personal message for me from the rabbi: 'Your son is going to be well. But one thing I want you to promise me. Whenever you see people in trouble, help them.'

"I returned home only to discover that my son's condition had already improved. His recovery was in fact both rapid and remarkable. None of the healers could explain his sudden recuperation. They had all relegated my son to an early death.

"This incident happened almost two decades ago and today my son is alive and well," Tarnowan concluded. "Ever since this time, I have revered Rabbi Paneth as a holy man and my son's savior. In his merit, I will do all I can to help you."

Tarnowan hid the Paneth family for two weeks,

providing them with food and shelter. When the Nazis became suspicious and started searching the woods, the judge sent the Paneths on to his cousin, who lived in a different part of the country and who agreed to hide them for several months.

Thus, in this way, both the judge's debt and the rabbi's injunction — intertwined as one — became fulfilled, and the Paneth family survived the war.

I was forty-five years old when my husband died after a long, brave battle with cancer. He had not allowed the illness to insinuate itself into his life; he actually worked at his job up until one week before his death. "It's not dying that frightens me so much as leaving you," he said. We had been blessed with a wonderful marriage.

The first year I grieved continuously. Although I seemed to be functioning normally, I felt a deep void and a constant ache in my heart. I was still reeling from my own father's death only twelve months before my husband's, and now a terminal prognosis had just been handed down to my ailing mother as well. On dialysis, but dying nevertheless, she moved into my home, where I would care for her over the course of the next three years. It was a very hard time.

It would have been easy for me to fall apart, but I was the mother of three children—two of whom were still living at home and depending on me. I was possessed by a strong sense of responsibility toward them and the knowledge that if *I* fell apart, they would, too. So I tried to pull myself together by seeking diversions for myself and by keeping up my spirits in different ways. I wondered quietly if I would really be able to continue living without my husband at my side, but I knew that for the sake of my children, I would have to try to go on.

After eighteen months of healing, I picked up the phone one day and called Mindy, an acquaintance whom I saw occasionally at PTA meetings and community events. I had been told that she, too, had lost her husband recently, and although she was older than I, she was a young widow like me. Because I was a year and a half past the initial stage of grief that she was just entering, I thought that I could be of help to her and ease her way. And we could share our mutual experience of widowhood and empathize with one another's feelings.

"We have a lot in common," I said, after initial and awkward greetings had been exchanged. "Why don't we go out to dinner and talk?" Beyond widowhood, Mindy and I discovered over dinner that we were similar in many other ways, and we became instant friends.

But although our values and backgrounds were alike, our temperaments were diametrically opposite: I was the more upbeat personality, she the more serious. I fought the heartache of widowhood more aggressively, while there were many times when she allowed it to engulf her completely.

Mindy was content to stay home, putter, and grieve, but *I* was convinced that this was a recipe for emotional disaster. So I made it my business to pull Mindy out of the house as often as possible and get her to do things with me.

"Let's go downtown," I'd coax.

"Please come to the theater with me," I'd cajole.

"I need someone to accompany me on a trip to Florida," I'd beg.

I just didn't let up. And thankfully, I was successful almost every single time in getting Mindy out of the darkness of her home.

Our friendship grew. We spent a lot of time talking honestly about the trials of widowhood, our respective happy marriages that had ended too soon, and the aching loneliness we shared. And about how we hoped that God would grant both of us the opportunity to marry again, if the right man came along.

Six years passed. One day, Mindy called me on the phone and said in a meaningful way that required no elaboration: "Hannah, you know this woman Lilly* who lives in town? Well, I just heard that her brother became a widower."

"Lilly?" I said dubiously. "I was in the same high school class with her ages ago. I wasn't really close with her then, and we're not friendly today, either. We're very different types of people. Honestly, I don't think any brother of Lilly's could possibly be for me. . . ."

"You shouldn't rule out good prospects so quickly. They're few and far between, as we both know. I hear he's a terrific guy. Let me check this out for you," Mindy offered.

She didn't falter or procrastinate. True to her word, Mindy immediately picked up the phone and called Lilly. "I hear your brother was recently widowed," she plunged right in. "Do you know Hannah? I'm thinking she'd be a great match for him."

"Well . . ." Lilly said hesitantly, "Hannah and I were never really friendly in high school, and we haven't kept up over the years, and we're not the same type. I don't know . . ."

"Look," Mindy persisted, "it's thirty years later. Why don't you ask around town and find out what kind of person Hannah's grown into?"

Mindy reported back later that Lilly had put out feelers all over town and had gotten good feedback, but she still didn't want to approach her brother at this time. "She says it's too soon," Mindy explained to me.

And I promptly forgot about the whole thing.

A few months later, my married son urged me to see a kabbalist (mystic/psychic) from Israel who was in town. "He's amazing!" my son enthused. "I went to see him with my wife, and he seemed to know everything about us. He gave great advice. I want *you* to go, too, Mom."

"Don't be ridiculous," I said, waving my hand in dismissal. "I don't believe in kabbalists. I would be embarrassed to go to a kabbalist. No way will I see a kabbalist . . ."

A few hours later, I was in his study, unburdening myself.

"I'm a widow," I explained. "I don't want to be alone for the rest of my life."

"Have you asked Rabbi so-and-so to help you?" he

suggested, mentioning the local matchmaker.

"Yes, but he doesn't know anyone for me," I answered sadly.

"Well, how about Rabbi so-and-so?" he proposed brightly, mentioning another man active in community affairs.

"I've been to see him, too. He couldn't help me, either."

We both fell silent for a long and uncomfortable time. *I'm going to kill my son,* I thought. *This has been a total waste of time. I don't need a kabbalist to refer me to matchmakers!*

As I rose to leave, the kabbalist said with sudden force and conviction: "Your fortune is that you are going to make a match soon."

I walked out of the room chuckling to myself, thinking, *Yeah, sure.*

An hour after I returned home, the phone rang.

It was Lilly.

"I'm a little uncomfortable doing this," she said, "but about half a year ago your friend Mindy called me and suggested that you might be interested in meeting my widowed brother. He's coming to town for a family wedding, and I wondered if he could give you a call."

A few months later, we were engaged.

Mindy was overjoyed for me, and thrilled that she had been able to serve as my matchmaker. In turn, I felt indebted to her for being so uncharacteristically aggressive on my behalf and for the pivotal role she had played in shaping my future.

But what of hers? I thought sadly. My happiness was marred only by thoughts of leaving Mindy behind, both emotionally and geographically. I had agreed to move to New Jersey, where my fiancé lived, and I knew that things could never be quite the same again between Mindy and me. The physical distance between us would discourage the easy intimacy we had known, and the emotional distance—the gap between a widowed woman and a newly remarried one—would also prove an obstacle. *I wish she would get married, too,* I thought wistfully.

Meanwhile, I was swept up in the whirlwind of my engagement and the flurry of preparations for the ceremony. My fiancé and I wanted the wedding to be a festive affair, but we didn't know what the exact protocol was for second marriages—which Jewish customs were appropriate second-time-around and which weren't.

"Since my uncle will be the officiating rabbi at the wedding anyway," my fiancé said, "why don't we just take a trip to New York and thrash everything out with him?"

My fiancé's uncle was a prominent pulpit rabbi, with many decades of distinguished spiritual service behind him. "If anyone knows the law, he does," my fiancé said with certainty.

As we rode up the elevator to the rabbi's apartment in a New York high-rise, my fiancé remarked that his uncle had lost his own wife about two months earlier. "They had a wonderful marriage," he remarked. "It's been a terrible loss for him."

I had expected a stooped, elderly man to open the door, so the rabbi's appearance—he was handsome, elegant, and distinguished looking—was a complete surprise. After pleasantries had been exchanged, the two men launched into an extensive discussion of the upcoming nuptials, but frankly I didn't hear a word they said. I couldn't concentrate because I wasn't present in the room at all. My mind was in a different city, focusing on a different person altogether.

Oh my goodness, I thought in sheer exultation. *He's perfect for Mindy. . . . She's going to love this guy!*

"Abraham," I said with a smile as we rode down the elevator together later, "I'm embarrassed to tell you what I was thinking of when I met your uncle."

"Okay, let me guess . . . you thought he was perfect for Mindy, right?"

My soon-to-be husband knew me well.

As soon as I got home, I called my friend. "Mindy," I exclaimed happily, "I just met the man you're going to marry."

"Yeah, sure," she said.

About a month after our wedding, my husband and I traveled to Israel to meet his immediate family—his parents and five different sets of uncles and aunts. The rabbi in New York was brother to them all, so I made it my business to emphatically say to each and every one of them, over and over again, until I was blue in the face: "I have the most wonderful woman for your brother. She's *perfect* for him. When he's ready, please ask him to take her out. When he meets her, it's going to be a done deal."

Everyone laughed and thought I was nuts.

Six months later, the uncle himself called me and asked: "What's this I hear about your wanting me to go out with your friend Mindy?"

The seeds I had carefully sown half a year before had finally borne fruit: My message had been faithfully relayed by every one of his brothers and sisters whom I had cornered and convinced.

"Listen," I said. "I know you're in a lot of pain, and you think you'll never love again. But this is the most wonderful woman in the world and believe me . . . it's a done deal."

He laughed and said he would give her a call. He wouldn't be able to travel to her city until the next holiday weekend came up in two weeks, he said, but he would call her now and make the date.

He called her that night and they had a long, satisfying conversation. So satisfying, in fact, that he was galvanized to call her the following night, and the next night, and the night after that. Each call was hours long, lasting well into the wee hours of the next morning. And finally, following two weeks of nonstop phone conversations that were escalating rapidly in length, intensity—and expense—they met in person for the first time on a Saturday afternoon.

I was beside myself all day Saturday wondering how their first date had gone. "Tell me already! How did it go?" I shrieked, on Saturday night as soon as Mindy got on the line.

"I'm embarrassed to tell you this," she giggled, sounding like a young girl all over again, "but we're unofficially . . . engaged!"

A couple of weeks later, they were formally engaged, and a scant few months after that my best friend became . . . my aunt!

In the Jewish tradition, it is common to present one's matchmaker with a gift of lasting value. A year before, I had given my friend Mindy a beautiful gold pin to thank her for making my match. And one year later, Mindy gave me a beautiful gold bracelet for making *hers*.

And now that she's moved to New York City, which is a mere hop-skip-and-jump away from New Jersey, and has officially become my aunt, we see each other all the time at family weddings, bar mitzvahs, and other occasions. And no matter what we're wearing at these affairs—suits, dresses, or gowns—there are two pieces of jewelry that perpetually adorn our respective wardrobes, two gems that we never take off.

My heart feels full each time I see my gold pin embellishing Mindy's lapel, and in turn, her eyes always light up as they rest on her gold bracelet encircling my wrist. We smile at each other in recognition, and our smiles are radiant with meaning and joy.

—*Hannah Stern*

The Jewish tradition has a beautiful word—the word *mitzvah*. Loosely translated, it refers to doing good deeds, observing the commandments, and making the world a better place for God and all of His creatures. As a Jew, I have been constantly reminded by parents, teachers, rabbis, and even my spouse and children of my Jewish obligation to perform mitzvahs. Throughout my life I have tried to partially meet this obligation by donating money to charitable organizations and by donating my time and talents to a variety of civic and religious causes.

Three years ago, I found myself in a difficult financial situation. I had to let my volunteer commitments slide, and then stop altogether. Yet I was still bombarded by the message from my family and community: "Do a mitzvah!" It was a difficult dilemma.

By profession, I am a speaker/seminar trainer. For years I have been telling my seminar attendees that when faced with a dilemma, the best thing to do is to brainstorm. Make a list of all possible options and solutions. Since this is what I advised others, it made sense to do it myself. I took a blank sheet of paper and at the top wrote, "Mitzvahs I can do when I have no time or money." I sat back, just waiting for wonderful ideas to come. But my mind remained as blank as my paper. About to give up and tear the paper to bits, I suddenly became aware of my radio playing quietly in the background. The announcer was inviting listeners to participate in important medical research studies at a local hospital. The time required was only one day a year for five years. Here was a mitzvah I could perform with little time available and no money!

A phone call to the medical center informed me of a nationwide program to screen volunteers for colorectal cancer. The purpose of the study was to determine whether or not screening for early cancer detection could reduce the number of people killed by cancer each year. I made an appointment immediately, pleased that I would do this mitzvah.

The screening was not pleasant. It involved enemas and an uncomfortable colonoscopy. Midway through the exam the researcher paused and said gently, "There is a small polyp on your colon. Call your physician and schedule surgery immediately. There is the possibility that the polyp could be cancerous."

With fear in my mind but prayer in my heart, I scheduled surgery. The polyp was removed and, thank God, it was not malignant. Following surgery, the doctor said to me, "It's a good thing you offered to participate in the research study and learned of the presence of this polyp early, before it became cancerous." But I said to myself, reframing his words, *It's a good thing I decided to do a mitzvah.* I thank God for the obligation of mitzvahs.

—*Gloria Goldbert*

*A*ndy Silver* was a senior waterfront counselor at my summer camp. To me — I was a thirteen-year-old girl at the time — he was the grownup who held the key to that magical building known as the boating shed. Andy was the one you asked when you wanted to take out a rowboat, and Andy was the one who had to be shown that you have a boating buddy, that your life jacket was fastened, and that you knew how to maneuver the boat. If you couldn't prove these things to his satisfaction — no small feat — you didn't get a boat. It was that simple.

My summer camp was run by a Jewish organization, and many of its activities focused on Jewish religion and practice and on the land of Israel. We learned Israeli songs and dances, collected money to plant trees, and had a Hebrew-speaking club. Many of the campers and staff had visited Israel and planned to live there eventually, and many were also religiously observant. In fact, it was Andy Silver who usually led the brief ceremony marking the end of the Sabbath every Saturday after nightfall. Dozens of us would stand silently while Andy chanted the ancient words, and I would imagine I could feel that Sabbath queen leaving us slowly and gently until her return the following week. To me these moments were the most special of all. I closed my eyes and listened to Andy's voice, forgetting that this was the same Andy whose canoe test was so tough I knew I had no chance of ever passing it.

The only time I saw Andy—aside from the Sabbath ceremony—was when my group had waterfront activities. One day, though, I found myself walking to the dining hall behind him. He was engrossed in a conversation about a work program in Israel that he was planning to join. "You have to be over eighteen years old," he told his companion, "and you have to be strong and willing to work hard. So I'm going to do it."

Then he paused for breath and said: "I'm going home!"

I was young and not very imaginative, and I couldn't understand what Andy was talking about. He was saying he was going to Israel and going home in the same breath—and I knew he lived not far from a major city. What was he really going to do? He couldn't be in both places at once. My curiosity finally won out over my manners, and I asked him.

He would have been within his rights to scold me for butting in, but he didn't. Instead, he tossed over his shoulder, almost offhandedly, the following words: "Israel *is* home."

Fourteen years later, I moved to Israel. Andy's words had resurfaced in my mind time and time again, and they were there to reassure me when I got off the plane and enrolled in a half-year-long intensive course in Hebrew. On my last weekend in the course—it was a live-in situation—I went to the nearby synagogue in Jerusalem for Sabbath morning prayers. Later that week I would have to leave the city because of my new job, and I was upset. I didn't want to leave the area. I had tried to stay with friends instead of at the dormitory on my last Sabbath there, but nothing had worked out.

I went into the synagogue and found it packed. Apparently there was a double celebration going on—a bar mitzvah and an approaching wedding. Because I had arrived late, I couldn't get a seat, and I stood in the back, hardly able to hear anything. But toward the end of the service, the synagogue became quiet as someone got up to make an announcement: "Congratulations to our bar-mitzvah boy, and *mazel tov* to our friend Andy Silver on his upcoming wedding."

Andy Silver? Had I heard correctly? The woman next to me saw my jaw drop open and asked me if I was all right. In a few whispered sentences I told her the story, and then waited impatiently for the final hymn. As soon as the last strains died away, I asked the woman to point Andy out to me. "Over there," she said. I looked in the direction she indicated and saw Andy for the first time in fourteen years.

I approached him, trying not to feel silly.

"*Mazel tov!*" I said, and told him my name. "Do you by any chance remember me?"

"Yes, of course," he answered. (If he genuinely did, I thought, it must be as the scrawny kid who had looked wistfully at the canoes but never dared touch one.) Then he asked me, in surprise, "What are doing here?"

With a grin I answered, "I live here." And I reminded him of the three words he had tossed over his shoulder to me during that walk to the dining room. "Do you remember? You said, 'Israel is home.' And now I'm here, thanks partly to you."

His eyes misted over a bit, and so did mine. We wished each other well, and then I went back to the woman who had pointed him out to me. "I wish I had known about his wedding," I told her. "I'm moving out of town this week and I don't know how I'm going to bring him a present."

"Don't worry," she said, with a smile. "I think you already did."

—*Rahel Jaskow*

"*S*o . . . where are you from?"

Rabbi Spitzer wasn't asking me where I lived now or where I originally hailed from. The elderly patriarch with the long white beard and twinkling eyes wanted to know my *ancestry*, my roots. What dynasty was I descended from, and what constituted my family tree?

He was Israeli and I was American, living temporarily in a Jerusalem neighborhood for the summer. He had met my husband at the Imrei Shefa shul in Har Nof and in a gesture of warm hospitality, had invited our family to his home for a Sabbath meal. Yaakov Moshe Spitzer was a stranger, but now he was trying to forge a connection, to find our commonality by asking me about my family tree. It was another version of the popular game known as "Jewish Geography."

I obliged him cheerfully. I told him about my father, who came from the distinguished Sanzer dynasty, and then my husband delineated his own equally illustrious lineage, explaining that he was a grandchild of the famous Berdictchever Rebbe. Rabbi Spitzer nodded politely but indifferently throughout these recitals. It was only when I came to my mother's side that a gleam of excitement shone in his eyes.

"Your mother is a Leifer!" he exclaimed excitedly. "Are you related to the holy Nadvorner Rebbe?"

"My great-great-grandfather," I answered.

"Then we are very much connected!" he shouted in glee. My great-grandfather was the Nadvorner Rebbe's *gabbai* (personal assistant) in Galicia, Poland, in 1870, and now their two grandchildren have coincidentally crossed paths, sitting together a hundred and thirty years later at a Sabbath meal in Jerusalem!"

He paused for a moment, and then, stroking his beard reflectively, he said: "So . . . let me now give you a gift, a simple gift, a gift of a story. As the Rebbe's *gabbai*, my great-grandfather was privileged to personally witness many of the legendary healings and miracles for which the Nadvorner Rebbe was famous. Some celebrated stories were shared with the general public; others remained unknown and unsung. Since you are his grandchild and a compiler of stories, I will now pass on one of these stories to you. This is my own great-grandfather's story and I will tell it to you exactly as he told it to me . . ."

୧୭

One of the things that everybody knew about the Nadvorner Rebbe was that he rarely, if ever, left the seclusion of his study. He was immersed in Torah learning day and night, when he was not seeing petitioners who streamed to him from all over Europe. He refused to allow himself to be distracted by mundane matters, and no one ever saw him venture outside even for a short walk or a breath of fresh air. His concentration was intense and he seemed utterly oblivious to his surroundings.

One day, I was working with him in his study when I heard a loud commotion outside. As he was always so engrossed in his inner life, the outside world had no effect whatsoever on the Nadvorner, and I assumed the noise in the street would escape his attention as usual. So I was thunderstruck when he looked up from his desk and asked me, instead: "What's going on outside?"

I gazed at him in astonishment. There had been many disturbances outside the Nadvorner's window in the past, and he had never paid any heed to them before.

But this time something was different. This time, he seemed to be actually troubled by the noises coming from the street, and he frowned in distress. In an action completely out of character, he gently suggested: "Maybe you should investigate?"

Outside I found a traveling gypsy with a dancing bear, a crowd of spectators surrounding them. People were throwing coins into the gypsy's cup as the bear danced for their entertainment. Itinerant gypsies were a common sight in Europe in those days, and there was nothing particularly riveting about the scene. I returned to the Rebbe's study and reported, "It's nothing. Just a gypsy and her dancing bear."

To my shock and amazement, the Rebbe got up and said, "I want to see for myself."

I was stunned. The Rebbe never wasted a moment,

and certainly not on idle matters like these. What could possibly be of such interest to him that he would interrupt his Torah learning now?

The Rebbe went outside and stood on the sidelines, unobtrusively studying the gypsy and her dancing bear. After a few minutes had passed, he approached the gypsy and abruptly asked: "How much do you want for your bear?"

Even the gypsy looked surprised. She stared at the saintly Rebbe with the luminous face. What would a sage like him want with a dancing bear? I, too, was exceedingly startled by the Rebbe's bizarre request.

"Well," she answered, "he's a very old bear and has only about another year of dancing in him, so I wouldn't ask for much." She then named a modest price.

"I'll get it right away," the Rebbe answered immediately, and hurried into his study where he kept some cash.

I blinked. Had a demon suddenly taken possession of my beloved Rebbe? Why was he buying a dancing bear?

The Rebbe paid the gypsy in full, and she left happily, not giving so much as a backward glance at the bear that had been her faithful servant for so many years. The Rebbe waited until she was gone, and then he looked the bear straight in the eye.

"Moishela, Moishela," he thundered in Yiddish. "You have danced long enough. You can stop dancing now. I have set you free."

The instant that the Rebbe proclaimed these words, the bear dropped dead at his feet.

My grandson, I want you to know that I witnessed this even with my own two eyes, and it was a privilege to be the holy Nadvorner Rebbe's *gabbai*.

And if you ever have the privilege to meet any of the Rebbe's descendants one day, please be sure to tell them this story, so that they too can know the greatness of their ancestor.

— *Yitta Halberstam*

After sustaining a severe heart attack in 1973, my grandmother sank into a deep coma and was placed on life support systems in the hospital. Her EEG was totally flat, indicating zero brain activity. She was hooked up both to a pacemaker that made her heart beat artificially and a respirator that made her lungs breathe artificially. But technically, as the doctors told me privately, she was basically as good as dead. "She'll never come out of the coma," they said, "and she's better off this way. If she did, her life would be meaningless. She'd exist in a purely vegetative state."

Even though she was in her mid-seventies and had lived a full life, I refused to believe that my beloved grandmother could simply slip away like this. She was too feisty, too vital to just disappear into a coma. My instincts told me to start talking to her and keep chatting away. I stayed at her bedside day and night, and that's precisely what I did. I spoke to her all the time—about my husband and our two small children, about other relatives, about her own life. I told her all the news that was circulating in Australia at the time. Anything and everything was grist for the mill. I also kept urging her to keep clinging to life, not to give up. "Don't you dare leave us!" I exhorted. "I need you, Mom needs you, your grandchildren need you. They're just beginning to get to know you. It's too soon for you to go!"

It was hard for me to do battle for my grandmother's life, alone as I was. During the time that she fell ill, I was her only relative in Sydney. Her daughter (my mother) was away overseas on a trip, and my only sibling—a brother—lived in Israel. My husband was home caring for our children so that I could take my post at her bedside. I stood a solitary vigil, but that was not what placed such tremendous pressure on me. What was enormously difficult was being asked to make decisions alone. The emotional burden was huge.

When four days passed with no signs of life flickering in either my grandmother's eyes or her hands, and no change recorded by the EEG, the doctors advised me to authorize the papers that would turn off the life support systems. I trembled to think that I held the power of consigning my grandmother to an early grave. "But she's really already dead," the doctors argued. "She's just being kept artificially alive by the pacemaker and the respirator. Keeping her hooked up to these machines is just a waste."

"Well, listen," I said. "It's Thursday afternoon, and in the Jewish religion we bury people right away. My parents are overseas—practically two days away—and they would certainly want to be here for the funeral. But we don't do funerals on Saturday, the Jewish Sabbath. The earliest we could do the funeral would be on Sunday. So let me call my parents to get ready to fly home, and I'll sign the papers on Sunday." It was all very cold and calculating, but deep inside, my heart was aching.

Meanwhile, I didn't let up. I kept talking up a storm, discussing weighty matters, babbling about the mundane. "Guess what, Grandma?" I gossiped. "You won't believe who ended up being your roommate here in the hospital! Stringfellow! Your next-door neighbor at home, Mrs. Stringfellow, was just brought in with a serious condition. Isn't that a coincidence? She lives next door to you in Sydney and now she's your roommate here in the hospital!"

On Saturday, I was at my usual post at my grandmother's bedside, getting ready to start a round of tearful goodbyes, when I thought I noticed her eyes blinking. I called a nurse and told her what I had seen. "It's just your imagination, dearie," the nurse said compassionately. "Why don't you go downstairs for some coffee, and I'll stay with her until you come back?"

But when I returned, the nurse was brimming over with excitement herself. "You know," she said, "I think you may be right. I've been sitting her watching your grandmother, and I could swear I saw her blinking, too."

A few hours later, my grandmother's eyelids flew open. She stared at me and then craned her neck to look at the empty bed on the other side of the room. "Hey," she yelled, "what happened to Stringfellow?"

By the time my mother arrived at the hospital the next day, my grandmother was sitting up in bed, conversing cheerfully with the hospital staff, and looking perfectly normal. My mother glared at me, annoyed, sure I had exaggerated my grandmother's condition. "For *this*, I had to *shlep* all the way home?" she asked.

Later, my grandmother told me that while she was in the "coma" she had heard every single word that was said *to* her and *about* her. She repeated all the conversations to me, and her retention was remarkable.

"I kept shouting to you," she said, "but somehow you didn't hear me. I kept on trying to tell you, 'Don't bury me yet!'"

After she was discharged from the hospital, my grandmother's quality of life remained excellent. She lived on her own as a self-sufficient, independent, and high-spirited lady and continued to live in this manner until her death sixteen years after I almost pulled the plug.

—*Judy Doobov*

"*Y*ou can't be a prophet in your own town," the Talmud warns, and I can personally attest to the truth of this saying, which may be somewhat akin to but less harsh "

I myself was guilty of this sin of omission when it came to my own father during one particular episode in my life. My father, Rabbi Zumer Rosenbaum, was a revered sage, known internationally as the Nadvorner Rebbe, and celebrated for his miraculous healing ability throughout the world. But when I suddenly found myself in trouble I turned to someone else for help.

In 1957, I came to the United States from Havana, where I had served as Chief Rabbi of Cuba. After Castro's ascent to power in 1957, the Jewish community scattered and fled, and it was time for me to leave as well. I eventually came to New York where I bought a house in East Flatbush to use as a synagogue that I named the Clarkson Avenue Shul. The building was *ah metzia*—a bargain—$20,000, inexpensive even then. The seller told me that the reason the house was so reasonable was because there was a lien on the property. He owed $40,000 in back taxes. However, he assured me, that since I was converting the house into a congregation, there was probably legal recourse to getting the debt "written off." I didn't know any better, as I was a "greenhorn" and naive about the intricacies of

American law. Only after I bought the property did I discover, to my consternation, what an expensive price tag it really bore.

Almost immediately after the transaction was completed, I received an ominous-looking official document in the mail, apprising me that I now owed $40,000 in back taxes. The letter left me reeling, and I was overcome with anxiety and distress. I barely knew how to make it around my new Brooklyn neighborhood, and now I would have to navigate the labyrinthine court system as well.

I discussed the situation with an acquaintance, who advised that I seek the counsel of a renowned Rebbe in Brooklyn. I met with the Rebbe, but unfortunately, he was not able to offer any concrete advice.

That night, I called my father and finally unburdened myself to him. He acted surprised that I hadn't discussed the situation with him before, and chastised me gently: "For *this*, you had to go to the Rebbe? Why didn't you come to me first?" Our conversation drifted to other matters, and the subject was dropped.

The following evening during Sabbath services at our synagogue, I noticed a new congregant slip unobtrusively into a pew. I meant to approach him after *davening*, but somehow was waylaid by other members of the shul. By the time I reached his pew, he was gone. The following Friday night, he was there again, and once more I vowed to personally welcome him to the shul, but the same unfortunate scenario repeated itself. The third week, I refused to allow myself to be sidetracked and succeeded in reaching his side before he left the synagogue.

"*Sholom Aleichem, Reb Yid!*" I warmly welcomed him. "I am Rabbi Rosenbaum and I want to welcome you to the shul. What is your name, my friend?"

"Arthur Goldberg," he said, shaking the hand I extended.

"And where are you from?" I asked cordially.

"Oh, around here," he answered vaguely.

"Are you planning to join our shul?" I asked eagerly.

"Sorry, no," he said. "I'm a member of another synagogue, but I heard your Friday night *davening* is beautiful, so I thought I would attend those services."

"And what do you do for a living?" I continued.

"I'm a lawyer," he answered offhandedly.

"Well, once again, welcome to our shul, and I hope to see you soon."

"Oh, definitely," he said. "Every Friday night . . . you can count on me."

The following Friday night he was there again, and this time I had a little epiphany. "Excuse me, Mr. Goldberg," I approached him, "I hope you don't mind, but I have a legal problem. Of course, I don't want to talk about it on the Sabbath, but would you mind if I called you on Sunday?"

"I'd be happy to help you," he said. "But don't call me, I'll call you. I have your number."

It was only after he left that I wondered how

and why he had gotten my number, when he didn't even know I would need to speak to him after the Sabbath.

True to his word, Mr. Goldberg called me on Sunday morning. I explained my legal predicament. "Don't worry," he soothed me, "I'll see what I can do."

On Tuesday, he called me again, this time jubilant. "It's all been taken care of!" he exclaimed. "You don't owe a thing. The back taxes have been erased from your record."

"But how . . . why . . . I don't understand," I sputtered. "How did you do it?"

"Well, I checked some public records in the Clerk's office belonging to various churches in the neighborhood, and I discovered that many of these institutions had also owed back taxes that were forgiven. So I argued that if these churches have been given this privilege, so too should one synagogue. So, you're free and clear!"

"I don't know how to thank you enough," I said ecstatically. "This is such a tremendous relief, you can't imagine. I am tremendously indebted to you."

"Happy to do it," he answered matter-of-factly.

"Well, I can't wait to see you to thank you personally," I said. "See you Friday night?"

"Sure," he said.

But I never saw him again. He never put in an appearance that Friday night, or the one following, or the one after that. He simply vanished.

I questioned my congregants anxiously. "Have you seen Mr. Goldberg? Do you know why he didn't come this Shabbat?"

"Mr. Goldberg?" they answered, mystified. "Who's Mr. Goldberg?"

"You know, the lawyer," I said impatiently.

No one had ever heard of him. I described him in detail, yet no one had ever seen him.

"But he was here! In shul! For four consecutive Friday nights!" I insisted.

Everyone looked baffled.

Saturday night, I ran to my Brooklyn telephone directory and called every single Goldberg listed. But no one knew a lawyer named Arthur.

Arthur Goldberg never returned to my shul and I never encountered or heard of him again. I even began to wonder if I had hallucinated the entire episode. But one day an official-looking document arrived in my mail advising me that the back taxes had indeed been stricken off my record, so I know the incident did occur—an enigma to this day.

Who was the mysterious stranger? Forty-five years later, the question still tantalizes me. Could he have been dispatched by my own miracle-making father, whose help I had initially spurned? It was, after all, only one day after I spoke to him about my problem that the stranger suddenly appeared. Was he Elijah the Prophet, or an angel in disguise? In my ninth decade, I know one thing: I know that in life, all things are possible.

—*Rabbi Mayer Rosenbaum*

young Private Winneger was with the U.S. Army as it marched through Europe at the end of World War II. His unit was assigned to a European village with orders to secure the town, search for any hiding Nazis, and help the villagers in any way they could.

Winneger was on patrol one night when he saw a figure running through a field just outside the village. He shouted: "Halt or I'll shoot!" The figure ducked behind a tree. Winneger waited and eventually the figure came out, and, assuming that Winneger was no longer nearby, started to dig. Winneger waited until the figure had finished digging and was once more on the move before he stepped out and again shouted: "Halt or I'll shoot!" The figure ran. Winneger decided not to shoot but to try to catch the furtive figure. He caught up with the figure shortly and tackled it to the ground.

To his surprise he found he had captured a young boy. An ornate menorah had fallen from the boy's hands in the scuffle. Winneger picked up the menorah. The boy tried to grab it back, shouting, "Give it to me. It's mine!" Winneger assured the boy that he was among friends. Furthermore, he himself was Jewish.

The boy, who had just survived several years of the Holocaust and had been in a concentration camp, was mistrustful of all men in uniform. He had been forced to watch the shooting of his father. He had no idea what had become of his mother.

In the weeks that followed, Winneger took the young boy, whose name was David, under his wing. As they became closer and closer, Winneger's heart went out to the boy. He offered David the opportunity to come back to New York City with him. David accepted and Winneger went through all the necessary paperwork and officially adopted David.

Winneger was active in the New York Jewish community. An acquaintance of his, a curator of the Jewish Museum in Manhattan, saw the menorah. He told David that it was a very valuable, historic European menorah and should be shared with the entire Jewish community. He offered David $50,000 for the menorah.

But David refused the generous offer, saying the menorah had been in his family for over two hundred years and that no amount of money could ever make him sell it.

When Hanukkah came, David and Winneger lit the menorah and put it in the front window of their home in New York City. David went upstairs to his room to study, while Winneger stayed downstairs in the front room with the menorah.

There was a knock on the door and Winneger went to answer. Outside, he found a woman with a strong German accent who said that she had been walking down the street when she saw the menorah in the window. She said that she had once had one just like it in her family and had never seen any other like it again. Could she come in and take a closer look?

Winneger invited her in and said that the menorah belonged to his son, who could perhaps tell her more about it. Winneger went upstairs and called David down to talk to the woman—and that is how David was reunited with his mother.

—Rabbi Kalman Packovsz

They were born into a life of privilege—and, as the times mandated (it was the 1970s), they rebelled fiercely when they reached their late teens. Sammy Westrich and his twin sister, Judy, had been raised by assimilated, secular Jews who had inculcated humanistic values into their offspring but eschewed religious life altogether. Perhaps it was only natural, then, that perversely, Sammy and Judy would become serious spiritual seekers, each attempting to find a way to fill the intense void in their lives. Sammy headed to a yeshiva in Israel, while Judy joined an apocalyptic cult in the Midwest.

In Israel, Sammy found the inner peace and spiritual bliss he had been seeking in a special school for returnees to Judaism. He felt fulfilled and content but his happiness was marred by his concern over Judy. Although she, too, claimed to have achieved spiritual fulfillment, he worried incessantly about the outlandish rituals, peculiar ceremonies, and grotesque acts of self-immolation she described in her glowing letters to him. Hearing that members of a similar cult had recently committed mass suicide, he became frantic to extricate Judy from the group.

For months, he besieged her with letters begging her to leave. But she was intractable.

"Can't you do something about Judy?" his parents

implored him, alarm bells going off in their heads as well. "Why don't you try to entice her to Israel? Even a yeshiva would be better than that cult!"

Sammy finally came up with a plan. He wrote to Judy: "I'll send you a round-trip ticket to Israel—*not* one way—and I'll pay for everything—hotel, food, traveling expenses, etc.—if you agree to spend just two weeks here. And the only thing you have to do in return is to attend *one*—just *one* class—at a special institute for women returnees. Deal?"

"Deal!" she agreed.

But the visit to Israel did not have the desired effect on Sammy's twin. The Western Wall, Rachel's Tomb, the Cave of the Patriarchs—all the holy places, indeed Jerusalem itself—did not work their magic on Judy; in fact, they left her cold. Nothing impressed her; nothing moved her; she failed to see what there was in Israel that so stirred her brother. "Can't wait to get back to the States!" she groused. "Too many Jews here!"

Sammy was frustrated but still hopeful. "Judy," he said one day, "remember the deal we made. You promised to attend one class at the Women's Institute. You've been here a week already, and you haven't made any effort to go. I hear that Rabbi Miller* is giving a fantastic Jewish philosophy class today on 'Faith in God.' He's famous in Israel; he's a charismatic and eloquent lecturer. You'll love him! So . . . how about giving it a whirl?"

"Nope," Judy said, yawning. "I don't feel like it

today. Maybe tomorrow."

"Judy!" Sammy burst into her hotel room the next day in an excited state. "A famous rabbi-folksinger from the States is going to make a rare appearance at the Women's Institute this evening. He's turned tens of thousands of Jews on to Judaism. Want to go?"

"I don't think I'm in the mood for a class today, Sammy. But thanks for bringing it to my attention," Judy said dismissively.

"Well—Rebetzin Halpen* will be addressing the Women's Seminary tomorrow. She's a very uplifting speaker. So how about if I pick you up and personally deliver you there for her class?"

"Could you get off my back!" Judy snapped. "I know I made a deal, and I promise you I'll keep it. I won't leave Israel without taking the one class I agreed to take. I swear—okay?"

But the day before her scheduled departure, Judy still had not fulfilled her pledge, and her brother was infuriated. "I spent thousands of dollars on this trip, and you're reneging on the deal!" Sammy shouted at her. "You're coming with me this minute to the Women's Institute and attending whatever class they're giving now! No ifs or buts!"

"Okay, okay!" Judy said, collecting her things. "I'm going; I'm going!"

But when they arrived at the Institute, Sammy's heart sank. The only class being offered that afternoon was on an intricate, complex topic—Jewish law—that lacked the stimulation or inspiration of, say, a Jewish philosophy course, and was probably too advanced for his sister. Worse, the lecturer teaching the course, Rabbi Rubinstein*, was notorious for being the most boring on the Institute's staff. Students had been complaining about him for years, but the administration hadn't had the heart to fire the elderly rabbi. Consequently, students gritted their teeth and endured the class.

Judy was no exception. "Boring!" she pronounced afterwards. "My God, all these minutiae governing human behavior! Is every part of your life legislated by Jewish law?" she asked.

"Judy," Sammy implored, "weren't you impressed at least by the ethics involved?"

"Sammy," his sister replied, "give me a break! I appreciate your concern and all that, but please leave it alone. I'm happy in the Midwest and that's all there is to it."

As Judy's plane took off the next day, Sammy watched it and cursed Rabbi Rubinstein under his breath. "Of all the luck!" he told his parents on the phone later that day. "The best teachers were giving fantastic, inspiring, uplifting lectures all week long at the Institute and she refuses to go to any one of them. She bypasses rabbis and rebetzins who have changed thousands of lives; she even forgoes a class by Shlomo Carlebach (the famous "Singing Rabbi")—and whose class does she ultimately wind up in? Rabbi

Rubinstein's, for God's sake! Rabbi Rubinstein, whom all the insomniacs in Jerusalem take, just so they can catch up on their sleep! What a disaster! What a misfortune! What a tragedy!"

Meanwhile, back in the Midwest, Judy was chosen one day to accompany the cult leader on a shopping expedition to town, and they were strolling down the city's main thoroughfare, talking animatedly, when the leader suddenly stopped in his tracks. "Hey, what's that?" he asked, bending over to examine an object lying on the ground near a trash bin. "Well, whaddaya know!" he exclaimed triumphantly, holding aloft a man's leather wallet. "Wonder if there's anything in it."

His eyes glinted avariciously as he tore it open to examine its contents. "*Paydirt!* There's a thousand dollars inside! This is my lucky day!" he shouted, pocketing the wallet without hesitation.

Judy observed his greed with widening eyes and a thoughtful look. "Hey, wait a second," she said slowly. "What about the person who lost the wallet?"

"Finders keepers, losers weepers!" the cult leader answered. "Isn't that how the old nursery rhyme goes?" he asked, flashing her a rapacious grin.

"But you're the head of a religious group!" Judy protested. "Why aren't you thinking about the poor soul who lost the wallet? He must be frantic!"

"He should have been more careful, now, shouldn't he have?" the cult leader asked, impatient.

"Look, I think you have an obligation to at least try to find the owner of the lost wallet and return his money to him," Judy insisted. "I think you have a responsibility to go up and down both sides of the street and ask all the store owners if anyone reported a lost wallet. And then, if . . ."

"Judy, are you crazy?" he said. "I'm not parting with this windfall!"

"Well, in that case," Judy replied grimly, "I'm just going to have to part company with you!"

Involuntarily, Judy Westrich had absorbed the heart, the spirit, and the essence of Rabbi Rubinstein's "boring" lecture at the Women's Institute in Jerusalem. No, she hadn't been enthralled by his talk; she hadn't been even minimally interested; but nonetheless, she had somehow managed to subliminally soak up every point like a sponge. Her unconscious on automatic, and probably against her own will, Judy had digested and assimilated every last word.

For the subject that Rabbi Rubinstein had taught that day that Judy had sat in on his class was *Hashovas Aveida*—the Jewish laws governing the return of lost property. Judy could not help but contrast the ethical, compassionate, and stringent standards mandated by the Torah with the amoral and unprincipled stance of the cult leader.

So she packed her bags and headed back to Israel, and she has been studying at the Women's Institute ever since.

Before the changes brought about by the women's movement, with all the crusades, campaigns, and legislation it inspired in the last century, getting married—for a woman, at least—was no easy thing. Especially in an unprogressive and undeveloped country like Syria. In the nineteenth century, no woman from a respectable home in Syria could hope to acquire a "good" husband without a decent dowry. Eternal spinsterhood was the usual fate decreed for a woman whose parents were unable to provide a considerable sum of money with which to marry her off.

Nizha Dweck, genteel and well-bred, could not venture into the "outside" world and search aggressively for a husband like her counterparts of the twenty-first century. As a single woman living in Aleppo in the 1890s, she had to wait for her family to make the necessary arrangements and act on her behalf. But her father—her protector, her buffer, her shield—had recently died, and her three brothers, to whom the mandate had passed, were not all that eager to raise the obligatory sum. After all, she was only a sister, not a daughter, and the amount of money they needed to gather was prohibitive. Consequently, they were delinquent and let both the matter—and poor Nizha—languish.

One night, the recently deceased father appeared to the oldest brother in a dream and chastised him sharply.

"You are not doing your duty by your sister!" he rebuked his son. "She is lonely and needs to get married. I want you to arrange a match between her and Moshe Gindi. If you don't, I am warning you, there will be severe repercussions in heaven, and your eldest son will be taken from you."

Trembling, the eldest brother awoke from the dream in sweat-drenched sheets and resolved to do his father's will immediately. The very next morning he began working to execute his father's orders posthaste. An appropriate dowry was collected, the Gindi family was approached, and the *shiddach* (match) was made. The events happened in such rapid succession that they would have left another young woman breathless or in shock. But Nizha was calm, composed, and serene throughout the unexpected and surprising turn of events, and she never once questioned her oldest brother about his sudden change of attitude. He in turn was embarrassed to share with his sister the fact that what had spurred him on was not intense interest in *her* welfare, but rather in his own son's. So he remained silent about what had transpired and didn't tell anyone—including Nizha—about the dream.

On the day of her wedding, however, he had an abrupt change of heart. He realized that it would bring Nizha intense joy to know how much her father cared about her—that he had actually traveled all the distance from the other world to ensure her happiness and well-being. He also thought that it would bring the nervous bride—for what bride *isn't* nervous on her wedding day—an extra measure of comfort to know that her father blessed this union and that it was ordained in heaven. To have this assurance would certainly confer on his sister a sense of inner peace and purpose—no small gift to receive on one's wedding day.

Nizha was in the midst of a flurry of preparations at her home when her brother walked in the door. She looked strangely serene and self-possessed for so young a bride. Nervously, he hesitated, wondering how to broach the subject. Finally he began: "You know, Nizha, this match is really ordained in heaven. . . ."

According to the script he had rehearsed in his head, she was then supposed to act surprised and say, "What do you mean?"

But instead, Nizha surprised *him* by saying, "Oh, I know that—you don't have to tell me."

He was taken aback by her supreme confidence. "How are you so sure?" he asked, puzzled by her uncharacteristic aplomb.

"Because just before I became engaged, Papa came to me in a dream and said: 'Don't worry about getting married, my dear, sweet Nizha. Everything's been arranged. Moshe Gindi will be your husband soon.'"

—*Ezra Dweck*

In 1980, I emigrated to San Diego, California, from Paris with my husband and four-year-old daughter, Rebecca. I had mixed feelings about the move, and my emotions were in turmoil since my own mother had died in Paris only two short months before. I was still in deep mourning, and the transition was difficult. Rebecca, however, adjusted quickly and easily to the new environment. In fact, her acculturation was so rapid and so complete that barely had we settled into our new quarters when she was already clamoring for the newest American fad toy—a Cabbage Patch doll.

Cabbage Patch fever had struck the younger set, and Rebecca was no exception. Echoing the nationwide cry of her new compatriots, she wailed: "I wanna Cabbage Patch doll!"

Settling into our new home was challenge enough. I wasn't sure whether I was quite up to the daunting task of finding a Cabbage Patch doll—a hot and scarce commodity in a city I barely knew how to navigate.

"Can you wait just a little bit?" I tried to coax Rebecca. "I'll get you a Cabbage Patch doll for your birthday . . . which is coming up soon. And you know what?" I proposed impulsively, brightening. "It will be a birthday present to you from your two grandmothers . . . Grandma Gilette (my mother) and Grandma Berte (my husband's mother), who died years ago."

But Rebecca was unusually tenacious for a four-year-old, and she grew increasingly insistent that I begin hunting for a Cabbage Patch doll now! Her vociferous campaign accelerated with each passing day. She was stubborn, determined, and unrelenting. Soon we were at a veritable standoff.

Weakening, I called toy stores all over San Diego, but all of them had long waiting lists and no merchandise. "*Everyone* wants a Cabbage Patch doll right now!" sighed the saleswomen in commiseration.

Rebecca, however, was not interested in excuses. "You promised!" she angrily accused. "You never keep your promises to me," she wailed, digging the knife in deeper, demonstrating a remarkable aptitude for guilt production for one of such tender years.

So I expanded my frontiers and made my quest international. I called my brother in Paris and implored: "Get me a Cabbage Patch doll. It's an *emergency*!"

At that point there were one million Cabbage Patch dolls in existence worldwide—male and female—each with its own name and unique history—but I wasn't picky; *any* Cabbage Patch doll would do. Frenzied, I contacted a friend in Montreal with the same entreaty. My brother and my friend turned their respective cities upside down in their pursuit of a Cabbage Patch doll for my daughter, but not a single one could be unearthed *anywhere*.

When I reported back to Rebecca, she was not

impressed by the fact that I had enlisted people on two separate continents to track down a doll for her personal pleasure. Her sniffles intensified as she repeated her by-now favorite mantra: "You promised!"

"Rebecca," I said, summoning up as much forbearance as possible, "you *will* get a Cabbage Patch doll for your birthday from your two grandmothers, I promise you. Just have a little more patience, and you will see, I will keep my promise."

Late one Friday afternoon, a friend called with exciting insider information: The Toys "R" Us branch in Chula Vista had just received a shipment of Cabbage Patch dolls. "Hurry!" she urged me frantically. "There are only seventeen dolls left and the shipment just came in!"

I called the store and asked if I could pay for one with a credit card and have them hold it for me. They were stunned at the audacity of my request. "These are *Cabbage Patch* dolls!" the sales manager said reverentially. "You have to come down yourself."

I flew down the freeway with Rebecca, and the saleswoman led us to a glass-enclosed case. "You cannot choose," she said with a haughty air of keep-your-hands-off-the-precious-Tiffany-jewels disdain. "You have to take the one I give you." She casually chose a doll from the case and handed it to Rebecca, who immediately began to wail.

"This is a *boy* Cabbage Patch doll!" she shrieked in dismay. "I wanna *girl*!"

"Sorry," the woman repeated firmly, "you have to take the one I give you." She was not yet familiar with Rebecca's unusual brand of persistence, but soon she would be.

Wails, shrieks, and cries emitted from Rebecca's skillful lips. She begged the woman for a girl; *I* begged the woman for a girl. Unable to bear the high decibel levels any longer, the woman finally surrendered, randomly grabbed a girl doll from the case, and feebly handed it to my triumphant daughter.

Clutching her prize joyously, Rebecca turned to me with a smile that melted my heart. "Thank you, Mommy."

"Oh, thank your two grandmas, instead," I said. "Remember, this birthday present is from them to you."

Saturday morning, Rebecca made her way to the master bedroom and climbed into our bed, where she cuddled with my husband.

"Look, Daddy!" she said, holding her Cabbage Patch doll aloft for him to see. "This is my birthday present from Grandma Gilette and Grandma Berte. Can you please read the tag around my doll's neck and tell me her name?"

My husband examined the tag that had escaped my attention and immediately went pale.

"Jackie," he turned to me, stunned. "Did you happen to notice the doll's name?"

"No," I said casually. "What's her name?"

"*Gilberte*," he said slowly. "The Cabbage Patch doll's name is *Gilberte*."

My eyes widened in shock. Now I understood why my husband had turned so pale.

My mother's first name was *Gilette*. *His* mother's first name was *Berte*. The two names combined produced the new name of *Gilberte*, the exact name of the Cabbage Patch doll that had been handed to my daughter randomly, out of one million dolls.

I had told my daughter repeatedly that the doll was a gift to her from her two grandmothers, and indeed, it was.

Ever since that day, I have come to believe that people who die stay with us in some form . . . always.

—Jackie Gmach

"*Stop* and smell the roses," a popular adage urges urban dwellers—the very breed that is too busy, too consumed by the maelstrom of city life to notice both the sublime and the ordinary of everyday life. Like many other successful businessmen, Ronnie Tawil leads a fast-paced, frenetic existence, but unlike many of his colleagues, he still possesses the ability to pause, notice, and take in the details. This human quality made him stop in his tracks one day and observe with full attention the plight of an elderly woman who seemed to be in trouble. No one else had noticed her.

Ronnie was rushing out of his house, headed for his car and an important errand, when he saw an unfamiliar figure on his neighbor's front porch. He knew his neighbor well, and knew that this woman was not a member of his family. At first glance, she appeared to be disoriented.

He was in a hurry, but she looked as though she needed help. Ronnie backtracked to his neighbor's house and approached the woman. "Are you all right?" he asked.

"I'm lost," the elderly woman responded helplessly. "I don't know how to get back home."

"Would you like me to drive you there?" Ronnie asked. The woman accepted his offer gratefully.

In the car, she gave him her address. After hunting for the location for a long time, Ronnie realized with a sinking heart that it didn't even exist. Sadly, it became clear to him that the woman was in the advanced stages of Alzheimer's.

After mulling his options, Ronnie drove the woman to the local police station.

"You can go now, Mr. Tawil," the desk sergeant said. "We'll take over from here. Someone will surely call for her soon."

Ronnie looked around dubiously at the noisy, grimy station, listened to the frenzied ringing of phones, beepers, and walkie-talkies, watched the overworked officers fielding phone calls and civilians simultaneously, and thought twice about leaving the vulnerable woman alone in this chaos.

"No, it's okay, thanks, but I think I'll wait here with her. I don't feel right about leaving her alone," he told the desk sergeant. "It just so happens that my mother is about her age. If she were lost or in trouble, I know I'd want someone to be with her." Despite the seriousness of the errand that had originally propelled him out his front door, he remained faithfully at the elderly woman's side.

"Would you like to eat something?" he asked her as they waited. When he brought her a yogurt and soda, she devoured the food hungrily. *Who knows how long she's been lost?* Ronnie wondered in sympathy.

About an hour later, a man called the station, looking for his lost mom. Ronnie was relieved that the woman would soon be safe and warm in her own home.

Exactly two days later, Ronnie's elderly mother had an

emergency of her own. Imprudently, Mrs. Tawil had driven alone to a bad neighborhood to perform some chores, and, when she returned to her car, had discovered that she had accidentally locked her keys inside. It was nightfall and the street was dark. Ronnie's mother glanced anxiously at the rough-looking characters who lined the streets. She was a ready mark—easy prey.

Just then, two young men wearing tank tops and menacing expressions advanced toward her. *They look like they belong to a gang,* she though nervously, and her body grew rigid with dread.

As they stopped in front of her, she got ready to hand over her purse. But instead of demanding money, one of them asked with a concerned expression: "Are you okay? You seem lost."

Flooded with relief, Mrs. Tawil explained her problem, and they promised to get her help. The two tried several gas stations until they found an attendant who was willing to come to her car and pry open its door. They waited patiently with her until the tenacious mechanic succeeded and she was safely behind the wheel.

"I don't know how I can thank you enough," she said appreciatively. "How much do I owe you?"

They shook their heads in adamant refusal. "Oh, no, we don't want money from you, lady—all we want is that you should stay safe," one of them replied. "After all, if *our mothers* were lost or in trouble, we'd want someone to help them out. You don't owe us a thing."

*I*n my student days, I traveled with a friend on a long trip to Europe, with a final stop in Israel where we both had family. In those days credit cards were not commonplace, so we took travelers' checks with us to cover expenses. It was hard to know how much to take in preparation for a two-month excursion, but my father assured me that in case I ran short, he would send me money through American Express.

When we reached Israel, my funds were very close to total depletion, and I confidently sought out the nearest American Express office. To my dismay, I was informed that the company's usual twenty-four-hour waiting period would stretch into something closer to a week. The office did not function on Friday afternoon or on Saturday because of the Jewish Sabbath. Since it was an American-based office, it was not open on Sunday, either. And it would be closed the following Monday as well because it just happened to be Labor Day. Thus a request put in on Thursday would not be answered until the following Tuesday at best. I hated the thought of having to approach relatives for a loan—which they would never allow me to repay—but it seemed to be my only recourse. What was I to do?

A short time later, I was walking down a street in Jerusalem when a total stranger approached and stopped short in front of me.

"Aren't you Mr. _____'s daughter?" he asked.

"Yes," I answered.

"I owe your father money and have been meaning to get it to him. Can I give it to you instead and ask that you pay him for me?"

It wasn't precisely the sum that I needed to cover all my needs, but it certainly went a long way toward helping me out in a pinch.

—*Dr. Sylvia Schonfeld*

*D*r. Abraham Twerski is a
renowned psychiatrist and rabbi who descends from a
long line of revered Hasidic leaders. Dr. Twerski founded
and operates a successful drug rehabilitation center in
Pittsburgh and has authored several popular books on
drug addiction and spiritual well-being. On the Sabbath
and holidays, he retreats to his home, where he invites
guests to share festival meals with his family. At these
meals, he relates remarkable Hasidic tales that have been
handed down from generation to generation—legacies of
the Jewish oral tradition.

During one Sabbath meal, after Dr. Twerski had
related a particularly striking tale, one of the guests
politely suggested, "Why don't you collect these stories
in a book? They're so moving, but I can barely remember
enough details to do them any justice when I try to
recount them myself."

Dr. Twerski was silent and looked thoughtfully at the
man. "I used to say the same thing to my uncle," he said
after a few moments.

Later that year, Dr. Twerski published his first work
of nonfiction stories, titled *From Generation to Generation.*

In Venice, California, Marilyn received a copy of Dr.
Twerski's new book from a friend as a thank-you gift. In
her thirties, Marilyn was divorced and raising her young
son, David. She had not grown up in a religious

household, and she knew little about Judaism, her religion. At the recommendation of a friend, she attended a few lectures on it, and she was so moved that she began to go to synagogue and learn more. Soon, she was incorporating some of the practices of Orthodox Judaism into her life, such as keeping kosher and observing the Sabbath.

Marilyn was a respected lecturer in sports nutrition, and she had been on the staff of the 1984 Summer Olympics. In June 1986, she had a speaking engagement in Atlantic City, and everything went smoothly until her return flight home.

On her itinerary, she had one layover in Philadelphia, then a second short one in Pittsburgh, where she would board a final plane to Los Angeles. The flight from Atlantic City to Philadelphia went without a hitch, and she was eager and excited to return home and see her son, David, who would be leaving for his first trip to sleep-away camp that coming weekend. She sighed. It would be the first time they would be apart for an extended period, and she couldn't help feeling a little wistful about it. *I guess my little boy is growing up,* she thought.

But as she exited the gate at the Philadelphia airport, she heard over the loudspeaker. "Flight 181 to Pittsburgh will be delayed fifteen minutes because of weather conditions. We apologize for any inconvenience."

"Oh, no," Marilyn said under her breath. She felt a flutter of panic and checked her watch. Luckily, she still would have just enough time to make her connecting flight to Los Angeles.

As she waited impatiently, however, there was another announcement: "Flight 181 to Pittsburgh will be delayed another twenty minutes."

"Don't they know people have connecting planes to catch?" she cried.

Her chest tightened. Now she really feared she would miss her connecting flight, and she ran to the reservations desk to see about other planes to L.A. But she soon discovered there were none that could solve her particular dilemma. As an observant Jew, she could not drive or take an airplane on a Jewish holiday or the Sabbath; Jewish law forbade it. A two-day Jewish holiday was to begin after sundown that evening, which was a Wednesday, followed immediately by the Sabbath, which would not end until late Saturday night. If she missed her flight, there was no way she could get home before Sunday afternoon. And her son was leaving for camp Sunday morning!

Everything was falling apart. She still had to help David pack—and how would she get him to the airport on Sunday? Even if he got a ride from a friend, how could she miss sending him off on his first long trip away from home? And where would she stay for the next three days—so she could properly observe the holiday and Sabbath? These thoughts played over and over in her head until they finally announced that Flight 181 was ready for boarding.

She fretted the entire way from Philadelphia to Pittsburgh, hoping and praying that she would make it. As the plane landed and arrived at the terminal, she grabbed her duffel bag and dashed to the exit, slightly crazed. She ran all the way to the connecting flight, but it was no use. The flight to Los Angeles had already left.

"Oh, no!" she cried aloud, suddenly paralyzed by her anger and frustration. For a moment she just stood there and sobbed, feeling the sting of life's unfairness.

After a few minutes, she'd calmed down and gathered her wits about her. She called her rabbi in Los Angeles.

"Stay in Pittsburgh for the holiday and the Sabbath," he advised her. "We'll help you with your son. Find a Jewish family to stay with."

Since she didn't know anyone in Pittsburgh, she tried to reach some local synagogues. But with the holiday approaching, their offices were closed. She tried a few other Jewish organizations. No luck. Panic began to overtake her again. She checked her wallet; she had almost no money. She had never felt so helpless.

Then, suddenly, the name Abraham Twerski popped into her head. He lived in Pittsburgh. Yes. Yes, she was sure of it. She remembered his name from inside the jacket cover of his book, *From Generation to Generation. He runs a hospital for drug addicts in Pittsburgh! I must find him!*

She took a cab to Twerski's hospital, spending nearly all the cash she had. She bolted inside and found Dr.

Twerski's office, but it was empty. She uttered another cry of despair.

Marilyn found one of the doctor's associates. "Please give me his number at home," she asked.

"I'm sorry, I can't do that," the associate replied. Marilyn explained her situation, but her frenetic, panicked manner only made the associate more nervous.

"Of all people, the rabbi would understand," Marilyn pleaded. "Please, you have to help me. I don't even have any money left for a cab."

Marilyn's distress was so genuine that the associate finally said she would call Dr. Twerski's son, who also worked in the hospital. She called him at home, and he arranged for Marilyn to spend the holiday and Sabbath with a family near the Twerski residence. Dr. Twerski's son arrived at the hospital twenty minutes later and drove Marilyn to the neighbor's house. She almost couldn't contain her gratitude and relief.

As he dropped her off, he wished her a happy holiday.

"And you too, happy holiday," she replied. "And thank you again!"

Marilyn's hostess greeted her warmly at the door, surrounded by the exquisite aroma of freshly baked bread. "We're delighted to have you," she said. "Come, let me show you to your room." She led Marilyn upstairs and left her alone.

Relieved but still worried about her son, Marilyn immediately called a good friend in Venice to make sure he would be taken care of and would get to the airport all right. Then she called David and explained what had happened. She concealed her own disappointment, reassuring herself that he was in good hands.

Then Marilyn lay back on the bed, exhausted and hungry, and began to relax for the first time in hours. She replayed the day's tiring events in her head. She freshened up and went downstairs. The house was full of holiday spirit, and the good cheer and smells of cooking were intoxicating. She lit candles with the other women in the dining room as they waited for the men to return from prayer at the synagogue.

The men arrived with great noise and abundant greetings, and the family sat Marilyn at a place of honor for the evening meal. The warmth and the joyous songs uplifted and enraptured Marilyn in a way she hadn't expected—creating a sense of openness inside her to whatever destiny had to offer. When she went to bed that night, she fell into a deep and peaceful sleep.

The next day, it was arranged that Marilyn would have lunch at the Twerksi's home nearby. After hearing of Marilyn's mishaps, Mrs. Twerski said, "There must be a reason for all this."

At lunch, Marilyn felt the magic of the previous night lingering inside her. Across the table, several men were engaged in various conversations, and one of them, Steven, began to catch her attention. He had light, kind eyes and a warm manner, and he displayed an admirable conviction in his beliefs. He was also quite funny. Every so often Marilyn laughed at one of his offhanded comments, and as the meal progressed, it seemed his lighthearted jokes were meant especially for her.

At the end of the meal, Steven offered to walk Marilyn home. They walked slowly, talking easily and comfortably. It was not long before Marilyn felt as though she had known him all her life. She was disappointed when they arrived at the house where she was staying, hoping for any excuse to continue talking. For the rest of the day, all she could think about was Steven.

The next morning, over coffee, she asked her hostess where Steven would be having lunch after the morning synagogue service. Marilyn arranged to eat lunch in the same place. But when lunchtime came, Steven didn't appear. When Marilyn made some casual inquiries about him, she found out he was dating someone. *Oh, how could I have been so wrong?* Marilyn thought. *Was I the only one feeling a connection?* She thought that perhaps the wine and song from the night before had deluded her, and she couldn't help feeling disappointed.

On Saturday night, Marilyn quietly packed her few things for her trip back home the next morning. The telephone rang. It was Steven.

"Hi. I so enjoyed talking to you," he said.

Marilyn's heart skipped a beat. "Me, too."

"I changed my lunch plans and came over the next day to where you're staying so we could have lunch together. But I guess you went somewhere else." Marilyn smiled, but decided not to say anything. "Are you leaving tomorrow?" he asked.

"Yes. First thing in the morning."

"Would you like to go out for a drink tonight?"

"Yes," Marilyn answered. "I would."

That night they went out, and their connection felt just as strong as it had at lunch two days before. And as it turned out, he wasn't dating anyone seriously. The next day he drove her to the airport.

When Marilyn got home, she was just pulling her key out of the latch when the telephone rang. It was Steven.

"Was your trip all right?" he asked.

"Yes. I just walked in."

Then he dispensed with further small talk. "I'd like to come to L.A. to see you."

The next week, Steven went to L.A. and not long afterward, Marilyn visited him in Pittsburgh. Five weeks later, neither of them had doubts about their feelings for each other, and they became engaged. After they married, they settled in Pittsburgh, not far from the Twerskis, and they had four children together.

But their fated match was set in motion long before fog delayed Marilyn's flight.

Who was the young gentleman who politely suggested that Dr. Twerski memorialize his Hasidic tales in a book? That gentleman was Steven.

—*Miriam Sokal*

In the summer of 2000, Judy Doobov of Sydney, Australia, was visiting Israel and was taken on a tour of the ancient synagogues of Sfad, the city of mystics located in the Upper Galilee. It wasn't often that a cosmopolitan visitor from Australia sojourned in this city more renowned for its veiled mystery than for any modern-day attractions, so Judy—with her lilting voice and charming accent—drew interest wherever she went. But it was the *gabbai* (caretaker) of the fabled Ari Shul who was most attentive of all.

"He couldn't do enough for me," she recalls. "He was most gracious. He showed me around and then pointed excitedly to a beautiful, ornately carved thronelike chair."

"This chair," the *gabbai* announced with special pride, "was sent as a gift to the Ari Shul by a celebrated Hasidic rebetzin from Poland who had it transported to Israel by sea. It has since become legendary in our country for being a fertility chair. Any woman who sits in it who wants to conceive does so. The chair seems to possess unusual powers and brings many blessings. So please, sit down in it and I guarantee you will have many many children."

Judy began to laugh. *I guess I should be flattered,* she thought.

"Heavens *no!*" she howled. "My dear man," she

started to explain as the *gabbai* insistently tried to steer her in the direction of the chair. "I am fifty-three years old! My youngest son is twenty-eight! Whatever would I do with a brand-new family at my age?"

The *gabbai* looked crestfallen. He so much wanted to impress her with the power of the chair, and was so sweet and sincere, that she actually felt guilty about spoiling his excitement.

So she decided to indulge him instead. "Tell you what," Judy said. "I don't need any more children, thank you very much. But I do happen to have a married daughter who has not been able to conceive. Does the chair also work for grandchildren?"

"Sure, sure," the *gabbai* said, immediately brightening. He smiled with contentment as she sat in the chair and chuckled to herself. It was a good joke that she would be able to recount to friends when she got back home.

But the joke actually was on her, because nine months to the day after Judy Doobov sat in the fertility chair in the Ari Shul in Sfad, her daughter gave birth to her first child in Australia.

—*Judy Doobov*

*W*hen you are a follower of a *Rebbe,* you defer to your spiritual leader's wisdom and expertise before making major changes in your life. Thus, when my wife and I consulted with our leader—the Lubavitcher Rebbe—about our desire to move to the neighborhood of Crown Heights, Brooklyn, it was not an unusual act. In fact, it was quite the commonplace thing to do. Many of our religious cohorts sought counsel and blessings from the Rebbe on a myriad of matters, and ours was among the most mundane.

It was 1970, when a personal audience with the Rebbe was still possible. My wife and I were ushered into his study, and we explained the purpose of our visit. Since Crown Heights was the center of the Lubavitcher Hassidic movement, we did not anticipate any real objection to be forthcoming. All we really wanted was the Rebbe's blessing and direction. We were a little surprised, therefore, when he didn't grant it immediately. Instead, he paused for a moment and stared at us hard with his penetrating eyes.

"All right," he said. "You can move to Crown Heights with my blessing. But I strongly suggest that you move right near a hospital."

Before we could ask for an explanation of this cryptic remark, the Rebbe moved on to other issues, and soon the audience was over.

As it turned out, however, the Rebbe's one directive was not as easily fulfilled as we had envisioned. Although Crown Heights at that time boasted some of New York's most prominent physicians and finest hospitals, it was difficult to locate an apartment *right near one*. And we had clearly understood, from the Rebbe's emphasis, that it was necessary to find a home in close proximity to a hospital. After much hunting around, we finally found an apartment located two blocks away from a small, seedy, second-rate hospital, not one of Crown Heights' finer institutions. However, we reasoned, the Rebbe hadn't stipulated exactly what *kind* of hospital we had to live near, and since this was the only real prospect we could consider, we went ahead and rented it. The apartment was in poor condition and we were somewhat uncomfortable living in such shabby quarters. Still, we had procured the Rebbe's blessing a second time, and felt sure that we had done the right thing. We settled in and began building a family.

Soon, Asher, our first son, was born. My wife's pregnancy, labor, and delivery were normal, and Asher was robust and healthy. We hired a baby nurse to assist my wife until she recovered her strength. A few days after she returned home from the hospital, my wife retired to the bedroom to nap and left Asher in the care of the nurse. Everything seemed to be going well, the day was developing as normal and routine. But in one split-second, life turned upside down.

"Asher's choking, Asher's choking!" I suddenly heard the nurse screaming. I rushed to the phone to call the police, while the nurse hurtled out the door in search of help. Before I could register what was happening, two policemen summoned by the nurse scrambled up the stairs, dashed past me, grabbed the baby, and darted outside to their cruiser. Everything happened so fast, in fact, that I didn't even have a chance to follow the policemen into their car, nor to ask where they were going. The sequence of events that had unfolded so quickly—in a mater of seconds, really—had left me dazed and paralyzed. Seconds later, as I regained my wits, I ran into the street to look for the police car, but it was long gone. A kind neighbor, seeing my distress, offered to drive me around to the local hospitals in search of the policemen, the nurse, and my son.

In a haze of tension and fear, we made our way first to Crown Heights' biggest and best hospital, where, we were sure, the police must have taken Asher.

But he was not there, and he was not at the second largest hospital in Crown Heights, either. We didn't even think of searching the hospital right near our home, because it was infamous for its inferior quality. *Surely the police wouldn't take Asher there.* I stopped at a payphone to call my wife to see if she had heard anything. She joyfully told me that Asher was already back home, safe and sound. Believing that there was little time to spare and that Asher's very life was at stake, the police had rushed him to the nearest hospital where he was resuscitated.

"It's a miracle he's alive," a policeman told us later. "Asher was blue when we arrived. Even an extra minute could have meant the difference between life and death for your son."

"We know the hospital is second-rate, but we had to take him there because it was the closest."

"Anyway," the policeman added, "you wouldn't believe this coincidence. . . . Apparently, there was some kind of teaching seminar being held at the hospital today . . . they're trying to upgrade their reputation . . . and just as we arrived, some famous doctor who specializes in pediatric breathing problems was about to leave. He was rushed into the emergency room to work on your son, and he revived him using some brand-new techniques. The staff said the doctor had only come for a short time, but it turned out to be the right time at the right place. The nurses tell me they doubt whether your son would be alive now were it not for this famous guy being there . . . Lucky break, huh?"

—*Rabbi Tzvi Bronshtein*

*R*abbi Charlop,* a prominent man in the Jewish community and fundraiser for a renowned institution, stood lost in the labyrinth maze of the World Trade Center on the morning of September 11th. He had an appointment with a Jewish businessman who had promised a generous donation for his cause, and in his excitement, he had forgotten the slip of paper on which he had scribbled down the exact location of the man's suite of offices. Thankfully, however, Rabbi Charlop did have the businessman's phone number on hand, so he picked up the phone and called his office.

"I'm so sorry to bother you," the rabbi murmured apologetically to the businessman. "I'm here in the lobby, and I've forgotten on what floor you're located."

"*Chas V'Sholom* (God forbid) you should *shlep* up to me. . . . I'm close to the top. I'll come down to you. Wait for me in the lobby, okay? I'll be right down."

The businessman darted out the door with the envelope carrying the donation. Just as he reached the lobby, the plane struck his building, demolishing the floor he had just left.

"*Tzedakah tazil min hamoves,*" the Talmud says. "Charity can save your life."

$\mathcal{I}$*n* the aftermath of the Holocaust, tense and fearful Jews waited anxiously in America for news of European relatives who had vanished in the maelstrom of the war. Thankfully, there were many resources that provided continuous updates, including the Red Cross, international relief organizations, and several Jewish agencies; and their offices were constantly besieged by desperate supplicants seeking information. Good tidings were welcomed joyously, sadder news brought grief and mourning. But the third possibility—no word at all—cast the seeker into a different kind of purgatory, one from which there was no reprieve.

Sam Burg, his brother Henry, and their sister Clara had fled to New York prior to the outbreak of World War II. Three brothers, a sister, and countless nephews and nieces remained behind and were eventually caught in Hitler's net. When the war ended, and the truth about the fate of Europe's Jews was finally revealed to a public that had been oblivious to its full horror, the Burg brothers joined the lines that streamed to the Jewish agencies for information. Sam and his brother Henry took turns standing vigil at the offices of HIAS (the Hebrew Immigrant Aid Society), checking the bulletin boards that updated the names of survivors and the facts that were known about their current whereabouts. Sam and Henry spent entire nights at HIAS, waiting for their family's names to be added to the bulletin board—but the wait lengthened into weeks, months, and finally, years.

Sam and Henry Burg had no way of knowing that their entire family had been wiped out, with the lone exception of their brother Usher, his wife, two sons, and one daughter. From a DP (displaced persons) camp in Europe, Usher had been desperately trying to contact his brothers in New York and tell them that he was alive. But none of the agencies whose help he enlisted were able to locate his brothers for him, and he had lost the scrap of paper with their respective addresses long ago. Usher had no idea where his brothers lived. Officials at the organizations he tried were sympathetic but ultimately unable to help. "Sorry," they said, "but Burg is an extremely common name in new York. It's like looking for a needle in a haystack."

Usher felt frustrated and stonewalled. But he was an optimist, so he decided to try to make contact himself. He did not know the English names his brothers had assumed on their arrival in America and he certainly had no sense of how large a city New York was. So, in his naiveté, he addressed his letter simply to "Mr. Burg, New York City."

In the 1940s—long before the advent of computers or automated machinery—mail was hand-sorted by postal clerks, and it was a daunting task. Envelopes that were inadequately or incorrectly addressed were transferred to the "dead letter box" and from there to the nether regions of the post office—never to see the light of day again. One morning, in the main post office on Eighth Avenue in Manhattan, John O'Hara* was holding in his hand a letter destined for just such a fate, when he paused and took a second look.

Wow, this is bizarre, he thought. *Burg, New York City . . . Whatever could the sender have been thinking? How many Bergs and Burgs are there in Manhattan alone? The sender must be nuts.* O'Hara was about to throw the envelope into the dead letter drawer when he stopped short and reconsidered. Of all the hundreds of postal clerks on duty that day and sorting mail side by side, he was probably the only one there who actually knew a man named Burg.

Hey, what about the Jewish guy who owns Burg's Deli in Harlem? Where I get those great pastrami sandwiches? I bet he'd get a kick out of this. Burg always kibitzes with me. It's about time I one-up him. I know . . . I'll play a practical joke on him. I'll bring him the envelope and say: "Guess what, Burg? Special delivery" He'll get all excited . . . for nothing. Rubbing his hands in glee at the trick he planned to pull on the deli guy, O'Hara removed the envelope and placed it inside his coat pocket.

That night, O'Hara sauntered into the Harlem delicatessen and reenacted the scenario he had scripted in his head earlier that day. "Here, Burg," he shouted. "I have something for you. It came to you at the post office . . ."

O'Hara expected a reaction: that was, after all, the point of his little joke. As the deli guy took the bait, tore open the envelope and read its contents, O'Hara waited for a broad smile, an amused chuckle, a chortle, or a grin. But his stab at humor seemed to have backfired, because his joke elicited none of those responses. Instead, after reading the letter, Usher's very own brother—Henry Burg, the deli guy—turned white and passed out on the deli floor, right at O'Hara's feet.

—*Rabbi Melvin Burg*

$\mathcal{A}$ *young* girl stood near her father on the quay of a Polish harbor, a steamer trunk at her feet. Out of her nine siblings, twelve-year-old Rose was the child chosen to be sent to the "golden land," America. Life in Poland was hard, hunger a constant visitor in her home. After much scraping and pinching, her family had saved enough for a single one-way ticket to the United States. And Rose, the youngest of the nine, was the lucky one chosen to go.

Her father hoisted the trunk on his shoulder and walked silently, his coattails flapping behind him. Rose could see the effort he was making to keep his emotions in check. The weight of living was apparent on the lines of his face, in the burning sadness of his wise eyes, and in the gray in his beard. His back, however, was ramrod straight, in seeming defiance of his tribulations.

With an involuntary sigh, her father dropped the trunk on the deck and turned to his daughter. A gray head bent over an upturned innocent face, as the father gazed deep into his daughter's unclouded eyes. He felt an urge to scream, to protest the cruelty of fate. How he longed to snatch Rose back home, to hold her as he had held her when she was a mere infant. Instead, he laid a trembling hand on her cheek.

"Rose, *mein kind* (my child), remember: God is watching over you every step of the way. Remember

His laws and keep them well. Never forget that more than the Jews have kept the Sabbath, the Sabbath has kept the Jews. It will be hard in the new land. Don't forget who you are. Keep the Sabbath—no matter what sacrifice you must make."

"*Tatte! Tatte!*" (Father! Father!)

Rose buried her face in the scratchiness of her father's coat, her slender arms wrapped tightly around him as if to anchor herself to all that was familiar in Poland. *Tatte* gave another heaving sigh. His straight shoulders bent over his daughter as his tears mingled with hers. A blast from the ship tore the two apart. *Tatte* bent down and hugged Rose again, squeezing the breath out of her in a hug meant to last a lifetime. Then he turned and walked down the gangplank, a stooped man, finally defeated by life's hardships. As the ship steamed away from the *shtetl* life of Poland, a fresh sea wind blew on the passengers preparing to start life anew.

For Rose, the journey was crammed with questions and uncertainty. Would her relatives really extend a welcome to her, or was she to be all alone in the new land? How frightening was the thought of a new life without her loved ones. As the ship made its entrance into New York harbor, the passengers stood plastered against the railing, shouting and clapping as they saw the "new land." Rose stood aside, shy and unsure. Would the new land fulfill its promise of hope, freedom, and riches? Would her relatives meet her there—or was she now homeless?

Rose did not have long to worry. Her relatives were waiting for her, solicitous of their "greenhorn" cousin. She was soon safely ensconced in their home. With her mature appearance and demeanor, it was not long before Rose found a job as a sewing machine operator.

Life in America was new and strange. Polish mannerisms were quickly shed—along with religion. Modesty, keeping kosher, and Torah were abandoned, together with the outmoded clothing and accent. Rose's relatives insisted religion was "old-fashioned": an unnecessary accessory in America. Rose, however, never forgot her father's parting words. She put on the new clothes her relatives gave her, cut her hair to suit the fashion, but never gave up on the Sabbath.

Every week without fail, Rose devised a new excuse for her boss to explain why she did not come to work on Saturday. One week she had a toothache, another week her stomach bothered her. After three weeks, the foreman grew wise. He called her over. "Rose," he said in a tone that indicated he only had her welfare in mind. "I like your work, and I like you. But this Sabbath business has got to stop. Either you come in this Saturday, or you can look for a new job."

Upon hearing of this development, Rose's relatives were adamant. Work on Sabbath, she must. They applied pressure; they cajoled, pleaded, and enticed. Rose felt like a leaf caught between heavy gusts of wind, pushed and pulled with no weight or life of its own. She was so young and vulnerable. She wanted to please her relatives. But her father's words kept echoing in her head. What should she do?

The week passed in a daze for Rose. Her emotions were in turmoil. *On the one hand,* Tatte *is not here to help me be strong. I so want to please my new friends. I want friends. I want to fit into this new land,* she reasoned. And then just as quickly came another thought: *On the other hand, how can I forget Sabbath? How can I give up the beauty* Tatte *taught me?*

"Rose, sweetheart, listen to us. It's for your own good." On and on went her relatives, until Rose's determination wavered.

On Friday, Rose walked to work, lunch bag in hand and head stooped in thought. She sat at her machine throughout the day, listening to the humming of the other machines as she absentmindedly went about her job of mass-producing. *Would it be so awful to do this tomorrow as well?* Decision time was nearing.

Whirr, bzzz, whirr, bzzz. The machine kept tune to Rose's troubled thoughts. What should she do—or was the question, what could she do? As the sun slipped over the parapets of the Lower East Side, Rose knew there was really no question. She was Jewish, and she would keep the Sabbath.

Sabbath in America was not like the warm day Rose had known at home. This week was the worst yet. She lacked the courage to face her relatives and tell them of her resolve. Instead, she left the house in the morning, pretending to be headed for work. Back and forth through the streets of Manhattan she paced. Together with the city pigeons, she rested in Tompkin's Square Park. "*Tatte,* this song is for you," she whispered. The pigeons ruffled their feathers. "*Yonah matz'ah bo manoach*" (on it [the Sabbath] the dove found rest). There she sat among the pigeons, singing the traditional Sabbath songs, with tears in her eyes and sobs between the verses. When three stars finally peeked out from the black sky announcing the end of Sabbath, the moon shone down on a weary girl and bathed her face in its glow. Rose had triumphed, but her victory would cost her dearly. She had no job and had alienated her family.

"*Baruch HaMavdil . . .*" (the blessing said upon the departure of the Sabbath). It was time to face the hardness of the world. Rose trudged homeward dreading the nasty scene to come when her relatives learned that she hadn't been to work.

As she neared home, a shout broke into her reverie. "Rose! What . . . what . . . I mean, how are you here? Where were you?"

Rose looked up at her cousin Joe, her expression woebegone.

"Joe, what will become of me? I kept Sabbath and lost my job. Now everyone will be angry and disappointed with me, and oh, Joe, what will I do?" The words tumbled out together with her tears.

Joe looked at her strangely. "Rose, didn't you hear?"

he asked gently.

"Hear what?"

"There was an awful fire in the factory. Only forty people survived. There was no way out of the building. People even jumped to their deaths." Joe's voice was hushed, and he was crying openly. "Rosie, don't you see? Because you kept Sabbath, you are alive. Because of your *Sabbath*, you survived."

Out of 190 workers, Rose Goldstein was among the minority of those who survived. The infamous Triangle Shirtwaist Factory fire on Saturday, March 25, 1911, claimed the lives of 146 immigrant workers present. Because it had been Sabbath, Rose Goldstein was not there. As her father had said, more than the Jews keep the Sabbath, the Sabbath keeps the Jews.

— *Goldy Rosenberg*

*I*f she could have emitted a low whistle of shock, there is no doubt that's what she would have done. But since she was a demure young lady of gentility and breeding, she gasped instead.

"The bill is . . . how much?" Chana Loeb* asked, her eyes wide in surprise.

"One hundred *shekels*," the Israeli dry cleaner repeated patiently, for the second time.

"I . . . I can't believe this," she stammered. "Twenty-five dollars for dry cleaning *one* dress?"

The elderly American woman standing behind Chana touched her shoulder in sympathy. "Dry cleaning is still in its infancy here in Israel, and everything's very expensive," she murmured in explanation. "But we don't say a word of protest, because just a few years ago there were no dry cleaners here at all, and we could only dress in machine washables. So, we're grateful . . . and quiet."

Chana turned around to face the woman. "I know what you mean . . . my Israeli friends have told me that dry cleaning is still a relatively new phenomenon in Israel. But I . . . I just didn't expect it to be so expensive. One hundred shekels is one-fourth my weekly salary here!"

A young man who was third in line had eavesdropped on the conversation and now chimed in. "Hey, if you think dry cleaning a dress is expensive, do you know how much I have to pay to get *suits* cleaned?"

He named an astronomical sum.

Chana gasped again.

"At least you seminary girls get some time off to work a little so you have some money. We yeshiva boys have to study all day long, and we have no chance for income whatsoever. . . . It's really hard on us!"

Subdued, Chana paid her bill and returned to the dormitory where she lived. She was an American studying for a year in a seminary, and this was her first real encounter with the high cost of living in Israel. In America, she would have paid less than ten dollars to dry-clean her dress.

As she busied herself during the day, the student's remarks began to haunt her. Chana was a compassionate soul, and she felt pity for the young men who had to struggle. Many of the foreign students came from wealthy homes and their parents subsidized their Torah studies abroad, she knew. But then there were those for whom study in the Holy Land meant actual sacrifice and penny-pinching. When she thought of what a struggle it must be for this group to cover the high cost of dry cleaning, she shuddered.

Earlier that week she had read about the legendary "Yossele the Miser," who performed anonymous acts of charity. Giving charity in secret was the highest form of giving, she had been taught.

"I know what I'll do!" she resolved.

The next day, she returned to the dry cleaning

establishment in her neighborhood and approached the proprietor.

"I'd like to do a *mitzvah* (a good deed)," she said, "but I need your help. I know that a lot of young men from the local yeshiva use your dry cleaning services, and you probably know them well."

The Israeli proprietor nodded.

"Well, I'd like to prepay you for the cost of dry cleaning a suit, and the very next guy who comes in who you know is struggling . . . tell him it's on the house! Okay? Just tell him the bill's been paid! Can you do that?"

The proprietor nodded again. "You are a nice girl," he exclaimed, impressed.

"But listen," she said sternly, "under no circumstances is the person to know that I paid, okay? It has to be a secret. Promise you won't tell!"

"I won't tell," he assured her solemnly. "Don't worry."

The proprietor kept his word. All that Thursday, streams of young men came in to pick up their suits, but he knew they were flush with cash and didn't need the young woman's hard-earned charity. He bypassed them all in his search for a worthy recipient. Late that afternoon, a young man finally entered whom he personally knew to be needy. So when Baruch* took out his wallet, the proprietor gleefully announced that someone had already paid the bill.

"What?" exclaimed the startled young man, "I don't

understand what you're saying."

"I said that you don't owe anything. Someone already paid your bill."

"Who?" Baruch asked, dumbstruck.

"I'm sorry . . . but I can't tell you that."

"Oh, but you have to!" Baruch pressed him. "I want to call the person and thank them personally."

"Well, yes, that's very nice, but the person asked to be anonymous. Just enjoy your good fortune. Next in line."

But Baruch didn't budge. "I'm sorry, but there's an issue here of *hakoras hatov* (the commandment to acknowledge and thank one's benefactor). I have to know who did this for me!"

"I can't reveal the person's name, I'm sorry. Next in line."

"I'm not moving until you tell me," Baruch persisted.

In other countries around the world, customers in line would wait passively or indifferently until the brouhaha subsided.

But this was Israel.

"Tell him already!" one customer shouted.

"Keep your promise! You can't divulge the name of the benefactor!" another yelled at the proprietor.

"Hey, I need my suit already!" a third shouted irately. "I'm going on a date in an hour!"

The flustered proprietor, unstrung by the numbers of impatient customers swelling inside his steamy shop, and drained by the young man's relentless persistence, finally caved in. He scribbled something on a piece of paper, folded it, and handed it to Baruch. "Here," he shouted. "I hope you're happy. Now will you let me take care of my other customers, please?"

When Baruch returned to his dorm room, he unfolded the paper and was surprised to learn that it was a woman who was his mysterious benefactor.

"Must be one of those wealthy Hadassah ladies on vacation," he thought. "Or maybe an elderly American woman who made *aliyah* (migrated to Israel) and wants to do a good deed."

So he was very surprised to hear a young, melodious, dulcet voice on the phone instead of the more mature tones he had anticipated.

"Hello?" the highly eligible Chana Loeb merrily sang out, when the definitely looking, immensely qualified twenty-three year old Baruch Stavsky* made the call.

And so it came to pass, that after he had thanked her for her good deed, they began to talk of other things, and their phone conversation lasted long into the night.

And today . . . they're engaged!

"*When* am I going to be the bride?" I wondered longingly, as I watched from the sidelines while my friends and classmates from Barnard College got engaged and married in rapid succession. In the 1970s, I was entrapped in a long-term but turbulent relationship with a man from whom it would take me eleven years to extricate myself. By the time I did, my biological clock had already started ticking, and I was sad that I had squandered so much time.

It was at a party that the ache for a child began to grow. A guest was attempting to navigate her way through the crowd with two babies (a set of twins) cradled in her arms, and I offered to hold one. When she placed the babe on my shoulder, I felt a sense of inner peace and bliss descend on me that I had never known before. When she later returned to retrieve the baby, I could barely bring myself to give the child back to her. That primeval desire that women the world over recognize had begun to throb painfully in my chest.

But the universe and God did not cooperate so quickly. It would be several more years before I finally met my husband, who was the complete opposite of the man who had consumed my twenties. We shared the same traditional religious and cultural values and clicked immediately. We were engaged one week after we met, and married three months later. When my daughter

Rebecca was finally born, I was thirty-five years old.

Rebecca, with her copper-red hair, vivacious manner, and keen intellect, had always had a protruding abdomen. We never gave it much thought until she was in first grade and had what initially seemed like a bad case of strep throat. Beyond taking the routine strep culture, our pediatrician insisted on doing a thorough general examination as well. When he did, he found Rebecca's liver and spleen to be extremely distended. Her spleen was ten times the normal size, and her liver was twice as large as normal. He looked grim as he advised us to see a pediatric hematologist immediately, and we knew he suspected leukemia. Less than two hours later, we were in the Pediatric Hematology/ Oncology Unit at New York Cornell Hospital, a place guaranteed to instill fear into the heart of any parent. After a battery of tests, leukemia was thankfully ruled out. But doctors were mystified. No diagnosis was handed down, and we still didn't know what was wrong.

Three weeks later, we had our answer, and it was a mixed bag containing both bad news and good news. The bad news was that Rebecca had Gaucher's disease, a rare genetic condition that affects primarily Ashkenazic (Eastern European) Jews; the good news was that a treatment for the disease had just become available, which, while costly, would allow Rebecca to lead a full, productive life.

My husband and I were stunned. During prenatal

counseling, we had tested for Tay-Sachs, a more common, better-known Jewish genetic disease, but we had never heard of Gaucher's, and I had no idea that I was a carrier. A gamut of emotions afflicted me simultaneously—fear, anguish, and shock among them—but my doctor chose instead to emphasize the positive.

"Look," he said, "I cannot begin to tell you how lucky you are. Just a little while ago, this disease would have been fatal. A Canadian woman lost three children to Gaucher's disease in the 1980s. But since this treatment was FDA approved in 1991, a child with Gaucher's can now lead a normal life and have a normal life span. It is the *only* genetic disease for which there is now a treatment. Imagine if you had given birth to her a few years ago, where there was no such treatment available. *Then* it would have been a tragedy."

Rebecca began treatment just after her seventh birthday. After two years on the treatment, her spleen has been reduced from ten times normal size to four times normal size. Her liver, which was originally twice normal size, is now only 1.4 times normal size. Rebecca can now participate in all sports, and as a matter of fact is the only girl on her Little League softball team, besides being a basketball star and a green belt in karate. She also has the highest grade average in her class.

It is only in hindsight that one can gain perspective and truly see the blessings and the miracles that permeate one's life. For so many years, I had felt lonely, frustrated, and angry, wondering if I would *ever* get married. But if I had married any of the boys I had dated when I was young—all of them Ashkenazic Jews—and had children in my twenties, there is a good possibility that my children would have had Gaucher's disease—a much more devastating prospect at that time—in the seventies and eighties—than now.

How could I ever suspect that what my parents regarded as a terrible misfortune—my not getting married early and not having a child at a young age—would actually turn out to be a blessing in disguise?

—*Rae Ellis Theise*

*I*n 1996, I traveled from my home in Israel to Johannesburg, South Africa, on behalf of Ohr Someach, a Jerusalem-based outreach organization for which I work. Although I had been sent there to run an outreach seminar for Jews from limited backgrounds, my primary duty at home consisted of manning the organizations' highly regarded Web site "Ask the Rabbi." During our five years of operation we had fielded more than 80,000 questions from Jews from all over the world, and the site usually got a few hundred hits a day. Because of its ongoing popularity, three different rabbis were required to monitor the site. Sometimes, it could be an intense experience, and I was grateful for the brief respite.

The South African rabbi with whom I was running the seminar, Rabbi Klastzkow of the Sunny Road Shul in Johannesburg, was a very friendly, generous, and hospitable man, and one day he invited me to a barbecue at Harteberspoort Dam, a scenic area about two hours away from the city. It was a massive park, with hundreds of acres of grassland used for hiking, boating, and picnicking. We chose a nice spot for our barbecue, and had begun to set up the grill when Rabbi Klastzkow noticed three backpackers traipsing nearby.

Spontaneously, he waved to them and motioned for them to join us. This was precisely the kind of generous gesture he was renowned for—almost an involuntary reflex on his part. Rabbi Klastzkow had no idea whether these backpackers were Jewish and he did not care. What mattered was that he had food and drink to share, and thought they might be hungry. It was the neighborly thing to do.

They approached us avidly. "Hey, would you look at this!" one of the exclaimed in disbelief. "Two rabbis in the middle of nowhere." (Our beards and yarmulkes must have given us away.)

"Please, won't you join us?" Rabbi Klastzkow said warmly. "It would be an honor for us to share our humble meal with you."

The three accepted gratefully, and we began chatting easily. During the course of our conversation we discovered that two of the three were Jewish, but, sadly, very distant and removed from their own culture and religion. They were highly assimilated and were illiterate in all things Jewish.

One of them seemed a trifle embarrassed by this lack, and offered sheepishly, seemingly as a form of compensation or apology: "Actually, I do have one connection to Judaism. I frequently use a Web site called 'Ask the Rabbi,' and I have somewhat of a relationship with this one particular rabbi who always ends up answering my questions."

Very casually, I asked, "What's your screen name?"

He looked at me, puzzled, but answered anyhow.

"Well, my friend," I said in great excitement, "I don't know if you're going to believe this or not, but you've just met him in person. I'm your rabbi."

The young man was blown away.

He had already been overwhelmed by Rabbi Klastzkow's kindness; no stranger had ever offered him the spontaneous hospitality that the rabbi had, and he had been moved by his warmth and unconditional love. But then, to meet in the boondocks of South Africa the one human being in the entire world to whom he spoke about Judaism . . . well, that just took him over the top. He was sure that what had brought us together was nothing less than divine providence.

I left South Africa a few days later, but learned from Rabbi Klastzkow that the young man had begun to attend services at the shul. Several years later, I returned to South Africa and "bumped" into him again. This time he was wearing a *kipa* and *tzitzit*. As a result of our encounter in the park, he had become an observant Jew.

—*Rabbi Mordechai Becher*

*C*hava Mindel Eidelstein
spent her weekdays behind a desk. A legal secretary
for the firm of Heinz, Mackintosh, and Speers, the
twenty-year-old alternated between various sedentary
activities centered on her word processor and her
telephone. Although she kept a pair of Reeboks in her
desk drawer, Chava Mindel rarely was able to make
use of them, even during lunch break, because her boss
was constantly saddling her with "just one more little
thing" he urgently required for an upcoming meeting.

Since she was able to get only minimal exercise
during the daytime, Chava Mindel was careful to employ
her off-work hours to maximum advantage. If she had a
choice between two subway lines, Chava Mindel would
choose the further station. If she had to shop on the
avenue, she would hike the four long blocks and not take
the car. On the evenings when Chava Mindel traveled to
Brooklyn to visit her grandfather in the hospital, she
would, naturally, take the stairs rather than the elevator.

Each Tuesday evening since her grandfather had first
become ill, Chava Mindel would stop at a dairy
restaurant near her law office, grab a quick supper, and
head straight to Maimonides Hospital. Through the
lobby she would barrel to the staircase, and up the steps
she would trip to the sixth floor.

But on a muggy Tuesday evening in August, Chava

Mindel had arrived at her habitual supper spot to find the doors shuttered.

CLOSED FOR RENOVATIONS, said a neon-yellow sign tacked to the window. WILL REOPEN SEPTEMBER 18.

And so Chava Mindel had headed off to visit her grandfather on an empty stomach. By the time she'd arrived in Brooklyn, the young girl's tummy was rumbling so menacingly, she decided to detour into the hospital cafeteria for a snack.

To Chava Mindel's delight, there was a tasty array of kosher food offered. The elegantly attired young lady (she was still in the sophisticated tailored suit that was *de rigueur* for employment in a top-notch law office) selected a salad from the industrial steel shelves of the self-serve cart and settled at a table to enjoy her meal.

At another table close by, a medical resident was sharing a portion of fries with a classmate.

"Cute chick, Jake," the freckle-faced Irish resident commented to his buddy as he nodded in Chava Mindel's direction. "Looks like a coreligionist of yours, wouldn't you say?"

In the sea of tank tops and sleeveless blouses characteristic of summertime visitors to the hospital, a below-knee-length suit coupled with a buttoned-to-the-last button shirt could lead to only one conclusion.

Yaakov Meir Zeller glanced in the direction his friend was motioning and was struck both by Chava Mindel's beauty and by her modest mien. The girl was placidly nibbling at her salad, unconcerned with the comings and goings of the other inhabitants of the room.

During his years at Maimonides, first as a medical student and then as an intern, Yaakov Meir had had ample occasion to observe Orthodox female visitors to the cafeteria. The single girls tended to come in knots of twos and threes. Most of them were modest in behavior, but occasionally the more audacious would allow their eyes to rove the length and breadth of the dining area, scoping out med students with yarmulkes on their heads. On locating a suitable specimen, these girls would primp, preen, and giggle among themselves. Occasionally, the really brazen ones would even come over and introduce themselves.

But the pretty girl in the navy suit took not the least notice of Yaakov Meir, and he felt just the slightest bit miffed. Imagine! So resplendent was he in his immaculate white lab coat, stethoscope dangling at just the right angle from the front pocket—and she was oblivious to his existence.

During the next several weeks, Yaakov Meir's path did not cross with Chava Mindel's, but he could not get the young girl's face out of his mind.

And then, just before Rosh Hashanah, Chava Mindel twisted her ankle while dancing at a classmate's wedding. An Ace bandage now encircling her foot, Chava Mindel arrived at Maimonides to visit her grandfather. She was tired and dispirited. For the first time, she decided to forgo the stairs and take the elevator instead.

In the lobby, Chava Mindel bumped into a former neighbor, and the two began to converse as they waited together at the bank of elevators. The elevator car that finally arrived was already half-filled with people who had gotten on in the basement. One of those occupants just happened to be a young medical resident with a yarmulke on his head.

"So, Chava Mindel," the elderly woman said in a very loud voice as the elevator began its ascent. "What are you doing here in the hospital just before Rosh Hashanah?"

"I've come to visit my grandfather," the pretty girl replied sweetly.

The older woman smiled broadly. "Oh, very nice, very nice. Such a good girl you always were, Chava Mindel. I remember the time Mrs. Harbush couldn't get out to the grocery store, she was so sick, and you were such a teeny girl, only eight or nine, but you did all her shopping for her. Even carried it up, all the five flights, right to her door! And when Mrs. Weitzman had to go to the hospital in the middle of Yom Kippur to have her baby, from shul you came home and watched her three little babies. I remember, Chava Mindel, what a good girl you were! So tell me, Chava Mindel, how come you're not married yet?"

Chava Mindel's cheeks flamed bright red. The woman, being hard of hearing, tended to speak in an extremely loud, shrill voice. Her last remark, in particular, had caught the attention of everyone in the elevator, and Chava Mindel could see smiles sprouting on faces all around her.

Wincing, but straining mightily to disguise her embarrassment, Chava Mindel turned toward the woman, who hadn't meant her any harm, and said in as light a tone as she could muster, "It isn't as if I haven't been trying to find my *basherte* (destined one). It's just that God hasn't seen fit to send him along yet." And with that, the door to the sixth floor opened, and Chava Mindel hurried out.

The next week, Chava Mindel's father, Rabbi Eidelstein, was in Maimonides, visiting his father-in-law. As he entered the hospital room, he passed two white-jacketed doctors on their way out, discussing the elderly man's prognosis.

"But you're not even on this case!" the first doctor was saying.

"I know," the second doctor admitted, "but I've been coming to visit Mr. Lithwick as often as I can and so I've taken an interest in his case. I'm kind of a friend of the family, Bob."

Rabbi Eidelstein's interest was piqued. Who could this Orthodox young doctor be, who said he was a friend of the family? The rabbi did not remember ever having seen the fellow before.

"Excuse me for being nosy," Rabbi Eidelstein said to the young doctor as he passed. "But I heard you say you were a friend of the family. How exactly do you know my father-in-law?"

"Oh," the young doctor grinned, "I really didn't know your father-in-law at all before I started to come visit him. But now that I do, I'm so happy that I've made his acquaintance. Mr. Lithwick is such a fine man, and he has so many interesting stories to share with me about the old days!"

"But then," Rabbi Eidelstein continued, puzzled, "who in the family is it that you know?"

The doctor coughed. "I sort of know his granddaughter."

"Which one?"

A crimson cast crept into the doctor's cheeks. "Chava Mindel," he replied, averting his eyes.

The rabbi was surprised indeed. "Well, I'm Rabbi Eidelstein, Chava Mindel's father," he said good-naturedly, extending his hand. "*Sholom Aleichem.* It's nice to make your acquaintance."

"*Aleichem Sholom,*" the doctor smiled. "You have no idea how pleased I am to make your acquaintance, too."

As Rabbi Eidelstein turned to go into his father-in-law's room, he took note of the name embossed on the white plastic badge jauntily perched on the young man's pocket.

"Dr. Zeller told me he's been coming to visit you," Rabbi Eidelstein said to Mr. Lithwick ten minutes into their conversation.

"Such a fine young man," Mr. Lithwick instantly enthused. "Not only is he a doctor, but a Talmud scholar, too. And so friendly! We talk sometimes for hours, late at night, when it's hard for me to get to sleep."

"Really?" Rabbi Eidelstein raised his eyebrows. He would have to ask his daughter how she knew this fine young man as soon as he arrived home.

But later that night, the rabbi was astounded to discover that his daughter didn't have a clue as to who Dr. Jake Zeller was.

"But the boy mentioned your name, Chava Mindel," Rabbi Eidelstein insisted.

Chava Mindel shrugged. She didn't have a clue as to how the young doctor knew her. But that is not to say Chava Mindel was not curious. In fact, her curiosity grew so intense that the next time she was at Maimonides she asked the nurse on duty (with whom she had become quite friendly over the months of her grandfather's hospitalization) to point Dr. Jake Zeller out to her.

Within minutes, Dr. Zeller was being paged to the east wing of the sixth floor. Chava Mindel lingered in the doorway of her grandfather's room to see, from a safe distance, if the person who would turn up at the nurse's station would be someone she recognized. But the young man in the green scrub suit who materialized at the nurse's station was a total stranger to her. As the nurse gestured in her direction, Chava Mindel, mortified, scurried into her grandfather's room.

"That's the girl, Jake," Rhonda the nurse winked at the tall, handsome resident.

"Thanks, Rhon," Yaakov Meir grinned. "I'm really indebted to you for your help." He fingered the mask in his pocket. "So tell me, Rhon," he said softly. "You're a woman. What do you think I should do now?"

The nurse smiled. "She looks like a shy one, Jake. Wait till she comes out, and then catch her on the way to the stairs. That girl *always* takes the stairs. . . . I can't figure out what she was doing on the elevator the day you saw her. And, Jake, when you see her, tell her exactly what you told me."

Yaakov Meir paced back and forth at the nurse's station for twenty minutes before Chava Mindel emerged from her grandfather's room. She was headed in the direction of the pantry to brew her grandfather a cup of tea.

And it was in the pantry where Yaakov Meir Zeller officially introduced himself to Chava Mindel Eidelstein, over a cup of Swee-Touch-Nee orange pekoe tea. The conversation went something like this:

HE: Hello. I'm Yaakov Meir Zeller.

Resounding silence, as she fusses with the tea bag.

HE: Can I help you with that? Get you a cube of sugar or something?

SHE: No, thanks. My grandfather is on a sugar-restricted diet.

HE: *(tapping his forehead in consternation)* Oh, how silly of me. I should have remembered.

SHE: *(clearing her throat)* Excuse me, Dr. Zeller, if I sound presumptuous, but could you tell me, please, how come you've been spending so much time with my grandfather?

HE: *(seriously)* I try to visit all the Jewish patients in the hospital as often as I can, Chava Mindel. I live right nearby, so even when I'm off-duty it's no big deal if I drop by for a while and alleviate some of the old folks' loneliness.

SHE: Oh, that's so sweet.

Silence.

SHE: *(no longer able to contain herself)* Where in the world do I know you from, Yaakov Meir, Dr. Jake Zeller?

HE: You don't.

SHE: *(eyes wide)* I don't?

HE: . . . yet.

SHE: Huh?

HE: You don't yet. But I hope you will. Soon.

SHE: *(confused)* But if I don't know you, how do you know me?

So he proceeded to tell her how he had first seen her in the cafeteria and how she had been on his mind ever since, but that he had had no idea what her name was or how to get hold of her or how to arrange a proper introduction. Then how stunned he had been to see her on the elevator several weeks later, on a day that he was not even supposed to be on duty but was substituting for a friend as a favor; how he had overheard the old woman lauding Chava Mindel's virtues while also mentioning her name; how she had stepped off the elevator on the sixth floor to visit her grandfather, and how he had decided to get to know the grandfather himself.

Chava Mindel listened carefully, enthralled. But there was still one piece missing from the puzzle.

"But how did you know which room my grandfather was in?" she asked. "There happened to be several older Orthodox men on this floor."

Yaakov Meir grinned. "It wasn't so easy to find out," he admitted. "But I'm a persistent guy. So I bought the biggest chocolate bar I could find and took it up to the sixth floor. Rhonda, the evening nurse, is a chocolate freak. And while she was tearing the wrapping off the chocolate, I mentioned, just by the way, that I was very eager to find out which room the grandfather of an Orthodox girl with long brown hair was staying in."

"So you came to visit my grandfather. . . ." She digested the information.

"You may not believe this," Yaakov Meir said sheepishly. "But the truth is, all this subterfuge is totally out of character for me. I'm really a very straitlaced, conservative sort of fellow. Almost a prune." And the young doctor sucked in his cheeks to approximate that withered fruit. Chava Mindel couldn't help giggling.

Yaakov Meir's eyes were dancing, but his voice turned serious. "I couldn't seem to connect with you through the proper channels, Chava Mindel, although I did try. The night I ran into your father, I was really proud of myself. I finally had your full name: Chava Mindel Eidelstein. So I went to a woman who is a professional matchmaker in Brooklyn and asked her to fix me up with you. But she said that although she knew six Eidelsteins in Brooklyn, none of their daughters were named Chava Mindel."

"We live in Queens," Chava Mindel said, smiling.

"Oh, I didn't think of that."

By now the tea was cool. Chava Mindel emptied the cup and prepared a second drink for her grandfather.

"So, now that we finally know each other," Yaakov Meir smiled, "would it be okay if I called you, Chava Mindel? I can give your family references from a multitude of rabbis. . . ."

"Yes," she said. "Now that I know you, mysterious Dr. Jake, it would be perfectly proper for you to call." And Chava Mindel winked slyly. "Even if I don't live in Brooklyn."

And so, true to his word, Yaakov Meir initiated telephone contact. Although the relationship had its ups and downs during the next several months due to Dr. Jake's erratic work schedule, by early spring the two were convinced that they were indeed each other's *bashertes* (soul mates).

Yaakov Meir Zeller proposed to Chava Mindel Eidelstein just before Purim, in the elevator of Maimonides Hospital.

—Shifra Kahan Weinberg

O*rdinarily*, Ari Schonbrun would already have been in his office on the 101st floor of the World Trade Center when the first plane hit, but he stayed home an extra ten minutes to help his son with his homework. So he was on the 78th floor instead, on his way to a bank of elevators that would take him up to the 101st, when he heard a tremendous explosion and the electricity went out. Acting quickly, he found the floor's fire warden and convinced him to evacuate. The closest emergency stairwell was filled with smoke, causing him and about fifteen others to grope around in the darkness until they found an alternate exit. Gingerly, they began to make their way down.

As they made their descent, Ari stumbled into a coworker named Virginia, who had sustained serious burn injuries in the blast.

"Ari, please don't leave me!" she begged. Faithfully, he stayed at her side and helped her labor down the stairs.

"I can't make it," she stopped. "I can't go on."

Ari knew that her slow-moving progress could mean the difference between life and death, but he couldn't leave her.

"Virginia," he cheered her on, "I know you're in terrible pain, but you're doing great! You have got to force yourself to continue on. I'm here, I'm with you."

"Ari, don't leave me," she cried again.

"I won't, Virginia . . . I promise I won't."

"Make way," he shouted to the crowds as they clambered down the steps, "someone is hurt here!" Though frantic and panic-stricken, the crowds obligingly parted, and finally, Ari and Virginia reached the bottom of the stairs.

Outside, as they gasped for air, Ari saw the first ambulances arrive at the scene. Virginia's injuries were serious enough to warrant immediate medical attention. As the EMT's prepared to place her in the ambulance, Ari—his mission completed—moved to an area near the burning building and stared transfixed at the horror unfurling. But as the ambulance started to pull away, Virginia's frantic voice summoned him back: "Please, Ari, please don't leave me. I'm so scared. Please come with me to the hospital."

How could he refuse? Ari ran back to the ambulance—the first ambulance to leave the World Trade Center—and jumped in. As the ambulance pulled away, the second plane hit. Ari turned back to glance at the spot he had just vacated. It didn't exist anymore. Twisted steel and shards of glass had rained down on the exact place where he had stood just moments before.

"See, Virginia," he later said. "First, I saved your life. Then you returned the favor and saved mine."

*F*or an activity at our synagogue-run summer day camp, we asked each child to write an inspirational message on a small piece of paper that also included the camp's phone number. The papers were then tied to strings that were attached to helium balloons. Following a ceremonial countdown, the colorful balloons were let loose, much to the delight of our campers. As the balloons rose to the sky and floated away, the campers squealed in glee, speculating about how far they would travel and where they might land. They chattered excitedly among themselves, wondering aloud whether people might actually find the balloons, and if they did, whether they would call and let us know.

It wasn't until the next morning when I arrived at my office that I realized how effective a balloon filled with hot air could be. Checking the synagogue's answering machine, I heard the following message:

"I don't know who you are but I'd like to tell you a story. My next-door neighbor and I have been living in this community for the past fourteen years. Recently, we quarreled about a trivial matter and it soon escalated into a full-blown fight. We were both too proud to apologize to each other, and with each passing day the situation got increasingly out of hand. My conscience bothered me more and more, but I just couldn't bring myself to do the right thing.

"This morning I was standing in my back yard thinking about our sad situation and how things had spun out of control, when I noticed a deflated balloon lying on the grass. I picked it up and read in amazement the verse: 'Love Your Neighbor As Yourself,' followed by your phone number. I ran to my neighbor with the balloon in my hand and we both started crying as we realized that God had sent us a message. We hugged and kissed and lamented the lost time.

"So while I don't know who you are or why you sent the balloon in the first place, I am convinced that God spoke through you today. Thank you for helping to mend the hearts of two foolish old women who sorely needed this sign, one that clearly came from above. . . . No pun intended, but it really struck home!"

—*Rabbi Sapotinsky*

A Jewish giant of a man, six feet seven inches tall, with muscles like an ox and blood dripping from his hands. This is not the kind of ancestor a family is likely to forget. So when David Sarlin, a college student, received an assignment to write a family legend, he immediately knew which story he would tell. It was a favorite tale of his father's and every time he heard it in the sunlit safety of America, David felt himself tumbling back into the nightmare terrors of the Old World.

As the story went, one Friday night, David's great-grandfather, Yitzak, was walking home from synagogue with his wife and daughter. Yitzak lived in the Jewish section of a small Russian village, where he eked out a living as a merchant and tried to avoid trouble. But when you're a Jew, trouble often comes looking for you. On this evening, a group of drunken gentiles staggered into Yitzak's path. Despite Yitzak's enormous height and bulging muscles, the gentiles showed no fear. Fueled by liquor and anti-Semitism, they shouted insults, spit in his face, picked up horse droppings from the street and hurled them at him. Worst of all, they menaced the women. Yitzak warned them to stop. They laughed and shoved his daughter to the ground.

With one mighty motion, Yitzak tore out a long piece of wood from a wagon and swung it at his tormentors. One drunk caught a blow to the head and collapsed; the others suffered massive injuries to their legs, their arms, their chests. Yitzak and his wife and daughter fled the scene, leaving behind a tangle of bleeding men. As they raced along the cobblestones, the clatter of their shoes was drowned out by the screams of the maimed and the dying.

"Yitzak, you must leave at once," said the rabbi, wringing his hands in the doorway of their tiny house. "The word is spreading through the village like fire. Everyone knows you did this terrible thing. Any minute the Cossacks will come to take their bloody revenge on you and your family!"

And so it was that the Jewish giant Yitzak and his wife and daughter vanished from the village where their family had lived for centuries. Shielded by the night, they fled across the border, never to return, eventually making their way to America.

This was the family story that David handed in to his college professor, confident that such a dramatic saga could not fail to please. But the following week, he was surprised by the stern look his professor gave him as he called out his name. "David? Please stay after class." The professor then turned to the girl seated next to David. "Karen? Please stay, too."

What could I have done wrong? David wondered. *Did my story offend him in some way? Did he not believe it?*

"Karen and David," the professor said, "do you know each other?"

They turned to one another. "I've seen you in class,"

David said. "That's about it."

"Well, maybe you should meet," said the professor. "You wrote the same story."

"What do you mean?" asked David, dumbfounded.

"Read this." The professor handed Karen's paper to David, and David's paper to Karen.

Side by side, they read each other's story. There he was larger than life, roaring through the pages of both: the Jewish giant, ripping the wood from a wagon, smashing his drunken tormentors to protect his family.

"I heard this story from my grandparents," Karen said to David. "How do *you* know it?"

"From my father," said David. "What town is your family from?"

"I don't remember," Karen said. "The truth is I don't know a lot about my family history."

The professor smiled at them. "You may not ever figure out how, but I'm quite certain you two are related. How else would you share the same family story?"

David and Karen never did uncover their family connection, but forty years later, David, who is now my brother-in-law, still marvels at this amazing coincidence.

"What are the chances that a stranger sitting next to you in class turns out to share your family story? The probability is so remote and yet it happened. It just goes to show you: All Jews are family. We just might not have figured out the connection . . . yet."

—*Peggy Sarlin*

*W*hen I learned that I was pregnant with my second daughter, whom we chose to name Elana, we set out to have her delivered at home by a midwife, just as we had done for her sister, Sarah.

Since we were living in Lancaster, Pennsylvania, at the time (home to a sizable Amish population) the task of finding one was not that difficult. We found a wonderful Mennonite midwife who had delivered well over 2,000 babies in the area before I signed on as a patient. The due date was established, the midwife secured, and my pregnancy proceeded without complication.

Finally, after when seemed like a interminable wait, my water broke. Ah, what delight I felt as the waters rushed down my leg and onto the floor. Perfect timing! It was on a Saturday, and Stephen was home with me. We'd get the job done before he returned to work on Monday.

Heavy contractions had begun for Sarah almost immediately after my water broke. Expecting a repeat performance, we moved into swift action. Stephen drove Sarah to a neighbor's house where she would stay until Elana was born. We called the midwife, who gave some instructions and asked to be notified when the contractions were ten minutes apart. We prepared our bedroom for the birth as we waited for the contractions to begin.

We waited, and waited, and waited.

The contractions never arrived, although every slight cramp or gas pain gave me renewed hope. Following the midwife's instructions, I drank practically an entire bottle of blue cohosh and swallowed an assortment of homeopathic remedies guaranteed to get the process moving. As I became increasingly desperate, I took to jogging my contorted body around the block and squeezing my nipples until they were sore—home remedies that should have brought on the contractions with a vengeance.

The clock ticked by. I prayed and begged Elana to decide to be born. And the clock kept on ticking.

We called the neighbors. "Sorry, no baby yet. Can you keep Sarah overnight?" I jogged around the block some more. And then I sobbed and sobbed, because dang it, nothing I did was working, and this baby wasn't moving.

The midwife called after several hours. State law required her to deliver my baby in the hospital if I hadn't delivered twenty-four hours after the amniotic sac ruptured. We had two more hours. I drank some more blue cohosh. I tweaked. I jogged, and then, I surrendered. I was going to have to deliver this baby in the hospital.

For a woman who has prepared herself for a hospital birth, this might seem like a minor inconvenience. For a committed home-birther like myself, this decision was devastating. I cried and shook all the way to the hospital and for a long time after my arrival. The doctors and nurses prepped me for delivery and hooked me up to a pitocin drip. After about five hours, I entered into the labor from hell, which would last, despite heavy doses of pitocin, all through the night.

My lovely daughter Elana was finally born, two days after my water broke, at 7:00 A.M. on February 5, 1996.

Only later, after she was home with me, did I discover the significance of her birth. We had chosen the name Elana merely because we liked the sound of it. February 5, 1996, was the Jewish holiday *Tu B'Shvat*—The New Year's Day of Trees. On this festive holiday, trees are planted in Israel and at synagogues and gardens all over America. The day is observed in joy, as a harbinger of spring. The holiday is symbolized by the picture of an oak tree.

The root of Elana's name in Hebrew means . . . "oak tree."

Elana wanted to be born on her holiday. No amount of blue cohosh, bouncing up and down, stimulation of Mommy's nipples, or even pitocin, was going to alter her plans. She knew what she wanted, and at 7:00 A.M., on her holiday, she gave birth to herself, with a little help from Mom.

A midwife can name a due date. An expectant mother can coax her body to cooperate. Doctors can pump pitocin into a woman's body. But when the baby wants to be born, he or she will, and there isn't a darn thing you can do about it.

—*Azriela Jaffe*

*N*ot many couples are fortunate enough to mark a golden wedding anniversary together, but my parents were doubly blessed with both good health and a robust marriage. Fifty years had passed since their wedding in 1912, and my four siblings and I decided to throw them a gala party in celebration on January 10, 1962. Because our families were scattered throughout the United States and lived along both coasts, we decided to converge on my sister Molly's home in Chicago—the most convenient crossroads for us all— where the festive event would be held. It would be a joyous occasion and a wonderful reunion, and we looked forward to it with great anticipation. I bought airline tickets for my wife and myself, spending a small fortune.

A couple of days before our scheduled departure from Los Angeles, I realized that my wife Helene*— normally a fastidious packer—had not yet begun her usual week-long preparations for the trip.

"Helene," I asked in surprise, "shouldn't you have begun packing by now?"

"Honey," she said slowly, "I don't know how to explain this . . . I don't really understand it myself . . . but I just don't feel like going. I have a gut feeling that I am needed here. Would you mind very much if I stayed home this time?"

In the past, my wife had always accompanied me on

family trips and had never once missed any of my relatives' celebrations. Typically, I would have put my foot down and insisted that she accompany me, overruling whatever misgivings she may have harbored. But this time, to my own surprise, I heard myself calmly say, meek as a lamb: "Okay, honey, if you don't feel like going, stay home." So, for the first time in the history of our marriage, I traveled alone to Chicago.

Meanwhile, after seeing me off at the airport and returning home that morning, my wife tried to call her mother and sister, who lived together three blocks away from our house. They didn't answer the phone, but that wasn't unusual: she assumed they were out shopping. Later that afternoon, however, when two of our sons came home from school, something made her ask them: "Did you see Philly or Jackie (her sister's sons) in school today?"

"No, as a matter of fact we didn't. Do you think they're sick?" My wife thought it odd that both children had missed school that day but had not picked up the phone in their home when she had called. Even if they were sick, she reasoned, they should have been able to answer her call. *But if they felt so badly that they couldn't even reach for the phone,* she thought, *then shouldn't my sister be home with them?* Nonetheless, no alarm bells rang in her head until she drove to a nearby religious school to collect our other two boys—the same school that her sister's younger sons attended.

"Did you see your cousins in school today?" she asked again. When they too said no, she began to wonder, but then quickly dismissed her foreboding as fanciful.

The strange confluence of events that day only began to take ominous shape in her head when she started dinner. A dish suddenly slipped out of her hand and crashed to the floor as a terrible revelation seized her at last: "Oh my God, they may be dead!"

Helene and our children jumped into the car and drove frantically to her sister's home. When no one responded to her frenzied bell ringing or to her wild pounding on the door, our son Ron rushed to the garage, where a spare key to the house was hidden. Helene's sister had shown her nephew the hiding spot one day, and he remembered it well. "In case of an emergency," his aunt had said.

As soon as Helene found the key and opened the front door, she began choking from the gas fumes that filled the house. Inside, she found her mother, her sister, and two of her nephews unconscious in bed. Her other two nephews were wandering around the house in a state of disorientation, dazed and zombie-like. When her efforts to revive her unconscious relatives proved fruitless, Helene called the paramedics, and the entire family was rushed to the hospital. After a time, all of them were resuscitated—with the exception of my wife's mother, who had sunk into a coma.

When Helene's sister and her sons regained

consciousness, they had no recollection of the incident that had nearly cost the entire family their lives. However, Helene's sister did recall that a plumber had come to fix the furnace the day before, and she surmised that he had inadvertently caused the gas leak that had overcome them during the night as they slept.

Meanwhile, my mother-in-law remained in a coma for five days, my wife never moving from her bedside. Doctors warned my wife that even if her mother did come of out of her coma, she would probably be in a vegetative state for the rest of her life. My wife refused o give up on her, and talked to the limp figure incessantly, making sure that she was constantly stimulated. After five days of touch-and-go, my mother-in-law's eyelids fluttered open one morning, and she was back with us, as sharp and lucid as ever. She ended up proving every single one of the doctors' predictions wrong, and lived to the ripe old age of ninety-one.

Although the incident occurred forty years ago, I have never been able to get it out of my mind. I happen to be a particularly stubborn person, especially when it comes to family. What possessed me—I who loved my parents so deeply and wanted to honor them so much—to suddenly exempt my wife from the trip without argument or complaint? And what in heaven's name had suddenly possessed her to insist on staying home?

My wife was the only one in Los Angeles who kept close tabs on her mother and sister. She was the only one who would have been aware that her nephews had missed school, and the only one who would have noticed that her mother and sister had not answered their phone for a long time. And she and my children were the only people in the entire city who knew about the spare key hidden in the garage.

If I had been stubborn and insisted that my wife accompany me to Chicago, a great tragedy would have occurred. Forty years later, I am amazed that my only response to my wife's reluctance to attend the party was one mild and very uncharacteristic sentence—"Okay, honey, if you don't feel like going, stay home."

In retrospect, I never would have forgiven myself if I had said anything else.

—*Joe Stein**

*R*abbi Shlomo Carlebach, one
of the most original and inspired Jewish personalities of
the twentieth century, had probably amassed more
frequent-flyer miles than anyone in history. As the
internationally acclaimed "Singing Rabbi" who reached
out to Jews everywhere in the world to reconnect them
with their heritage, he literally crisscrossed the globe several times a year. He was a familiar and beloved figure to
flight attendants and pilots on almost every major airline
in the United States, and he knew many of them by name.

On one of his flights, Shlomo was served by a
blonde, blue-eyed flight attendant who evoked his
curiosity because she radiated an unusual purity. He was
impressed by her sweetness and wanted to find out more
about her, but the plane was extremely crowded, and the
attendants seemed overburdened by their duties. They
rushed up and down the cabin dispensing food and
drink, and could barely exchange more than a few brief
words with each passenger. It wasn't the right time for a
long, cozy chat, Shlomo sensed correctly. Consequently,
all her knew about her was her name—Kathy—the kind
of name that matched her all-American fresh-faced
beauty and patrician, blue-blood looks.

Shlomo was in fact so sure that Kathy was probably
descended from the original Mayflower crew that he got
a bit of a shock when he passed the galley an hour into

his flight. There stood Kathy the WASP praying from a *siddur* (a Jewish prayer book)! He waited quietly until she had completed her prayers and then approached her.

"Holy sister!" he exclaimed effusively (his usual greeting), "you're an angel from heaven. But what are you doing? You're not Jewish, are you?"

Kathy explained that although her parents weren't Jewish (as Shlomo had suspected), she had always been inexplicably drawn to Judaism. "I have no idea where this strange and deep love comes from," she confessed, "but it has always been so compelling in my life that I recently converted."

Kathy told Shlomo that she had studied for years with an Orthodox Jewish rabbi, had undergone a conversion, and was now a practicing Jew. Shlomo and Kathy conversed at length, until a passenger called for her assistance and Shlomo returned to his seat.

Several minutes later, Kathy approached Shlomo tentatively. "Since you're a rabbi, maybe you can help me with a problem."

"It will be my honor and privilege to be of any assistance, holy sister," Shlomo rejoined in his usual expansive way.

"Well, here's my problem . . ." Kathy began hesitantly. "I'm in love with a Jewish man whose parents—although not religious in the slightest— strongly object to him marrying a convert. They've been carrying on something terrible, screaming and crying and threatening to disown him if we marry. We love each other very much, but he is also devoted to his parents, and he doesn't want to cause them grief. As a result he's terribly torn. The whole thing's incredibly ironic because I'm more religious than his parents! Nonetheless, I'm fearful that he's going to cave in under the pressure and call the engagement off. Is there anything you can do to help me?"

"I will try my best to help you," Shlomo promised. "Give me the phone number of your fiancé's parents, and I'll call them as soon as I get into my hotel. I will do my utmost to convince them to bless, not oppose, your marriage."

When Shlomo reached the father of Kathy's fiancé by phone, he found him hostile and unreceptive. Despite his best attempts to make the father listen to reason, Shlomo found himself making little headway. His pleas fell on deaf ears. But Shlomo was not one to give up easily. He persisted, as the father grew increasingly irate. Finally, the man snapped: "Listen here, I'm a Holocaust survivor, and because of what God did to the Jewish people, I have become alienated from Judaism, but still, if my son marries a non-Jewish woman, I'll kill him!" Shlomo soon realized that meaningful dialogue with the father was impossible and bade him goodbye. He then reached for the phone to call Kathy and report, regretfully, on his lack of success.

But it was Kathy's father, instead, who answered the

phone, and he too was antagonistic. He was angry with Shlomo for attempting to mediate between the two families and castigated him for his "interference." Silently absorbing the torrent of abuse, Shlomo responded—not with sharp words of his own but with the gentle lesson of a Talmudic tale instead.

Now that God has finished creating the world, the Talmud asks, *what does He do all day?* The Talmud answers that God spends one third of his day making matches! "So," Shlomo said humorously, "I'm just trying to give God a little help in his work! Obviously, your daughter and her fiancé love each other very much. Wouldn't it be a terrible shame if they did *not* get married?"

Something in Shlomo's voice must have touched the man, because he began to cry. "I will tell you a secret that nobody else knows," he told Shlomo, "and until your call, I thought I would never share it in my lifetime. My wife and I are not really Christians . . . we are Jews. We are, in fact, Holocaust survivors, and because of what God did to the Jews we came to hate our religion and renounced our heritage. We never officially converted, but we pretended we were Christian and raised our children as secularists. To this day, they don't know the truth about who they really are."

"But if this is the case," Shlomo responded, "and Kathy is actually Jewish by birth, then there is no problem! Her fiancé's father objects to her non-Jewish parentage. If you will tell her the truth, the obstacles

barring the way to this marriage will be removed."
Kathy's father agreed to tell her, and Shlomo spent the
next few hours on the phone, making a flurry of calls
between the two sets of parents. Finally, he arranged for
them to meet in his hotel room the next day.

When the two fathers were formally introduced and
rose to shake hands, both blanched simultaneously—in
shock and recognition. A series of varying emotions—
confusion, astonishment, pain, and awe—flitted across
both their faces in rapid succession.

"Herschel!" shouted one in jubilation.

"Yankel!" yelled the other in joy.

"You're *alive!*" both screamed at the same time.

To the bewilderment of everyone else in the room,
the two men fell into each other's arms and cried.

"We were best friends in yeshiva before the war!"
they sobbed in explanation to their wives and children.
"We learned Talmud together—we were learning
partners . . . But I was sure you were *dead!*" they
exclaimed simultaneously, looking at one another in a
mixture of both anguish and wonder.

So, the first-time meeting between the parents that
Shlomo had arranged so apprehensively did not turn out
quite as he had envisioned. It metamorphosed into a
tremulous and tearful reunion instead. Floodgates
opened, and reminiscences were invoked of a long-lost
era, forever gone. The two men spoke of their youth with
sorrow, nostalgia, and yearning. Finally, one looked at

the other and said with a crooked, funny smile: "Do you remember the fanciful pact we once made, as we dreamed about the future?"

The other laughed delightedly in recollection. "Why, yes I do! How strange, how very strange!" he murmured, as he turned to Kathy and her fiancé to elaborate.

"This is as strange as a Hasidic tale," he said, "but I promise it is true. When we were yeshiva boys together, we promised we would forever be friends We wanted our destinies to always be linked; we couldn't imagine a future apart. So, to solidify our friendship, one day we whimsically pledged that when we would marry and have children, we would betroth them to one another. And it seems that even though *we* forgot this pledge, God did not. Against all odds, the two of you met each other, fell in love, and fulfilled our vows for us."

*M*y friend Chave and I have a semi-regular tradition of going out for dinner during Hanukkah. She is strict about not eating until she has lit the holiday candles so I ended up kindling the menorah at our table in a mid-Manhattan kosher restaurant a few years ago.

This year, however, we weren't taking any chances. She brought a small menorah and the proper number of candles to work. I intended to meet her at the office and light them there before we set off for a museum. But her boss vetoed that idea—it would be a fire hazard.

So we went to the museum—in Soho, a trendy Manhattan neighborhood—with our holiday paraphernalia in a plastic bag. After touring the museum, we decided to go uptown to dinner. But first we needed to find somewhere to light the candles—maybe tonight's restaurant wouldn't let us.

Where to do it? In an alley? In a park? On top of a mailbox? We intended to leave the aluminum menorah behind, for passersby to see, so our only concerns were the wind (we didn't want the flames to blow out immediately) and safety (we didn't want to cause a fire).

A walk of several blocks turned up no appropriate site. Then we turned left on a side street—a dark street lined with auto repair shops with employees still inside at work. In the corner of a parking lot, in front of the shops, was a small dumpster. It was closed, with a level top, and out of the wind.

We walked in an open door and explained our predicament to a mechanic, obviously non-Jewish. Could we light our holiday candles atop the dumpster?

"It's not mine," he said. "You'll have to ask the owner of the repair shop down the block."

The door to the repair shop was closed. Chave and I looked in. The owner, seeing us, raised the sliding door. What did we want? We explained.

The owner was muscular, his bare head and bare arms open to the wind. *He'll tell us to get lost,* I feared. Instead, he said: "You can't light the candles around garbage," and beckoned us inside.

I thought his accent sounded familiar.

Koby was a sabra (a native Israeli).

He had a picture of the Lubavitcher Rebbe on his wall. He pointed to a *mezuzah* (the Jewish amulet traditionally placed on doorposts), to the right of the sliding door, that we had not noticed.

Koby cleared some papers from a counter. I brought out the menorah and started to insert the six candles. "It's left to right," Koby said, properly correcting me.

He looked for a *kipa* (a yarmulke) to cover his head. I offered my cap, underneath which I already had a *kipa*.

He answered "Amen" to my blessings, showed me a Hebrew *haggadah* (special holy book for the Passover seder) that he, for some reason, kept in his office, and, upon seeing my delight, gave it to me, first signing it.

He thanked us profusely for giving him the chance to do a mitzvah.

He wished us *Chag Sameach* (Happy Holiday), walked us outside, and drove back to Brooklyn—to his Torah class.

—Steve Lipman

There are chairs and a cozy sofa where you can sit and relax while waiting your turn at Georgie's, but no one ever does.

Instead of leafing through a magazine or browsing the pages of many catalogues displayed on the adjoining tables, most of us jump to our feet and hover around Georgie, watching in awe as her nimble fingers work their special magic.

Georgie is a renowned *sheitelmacher* (wig stylist) and works on Orthodox Jewish women who cover their hair. Her artistry had made her world-famous, the subject of a *New York Times* piece, and the object of our admiration. So, if we're early for an appointment, or if she's simply running late, we mill around the area where she's working and chat. Georgie seems to attract an especially diversified clientele, and there's always someone stimulating to talk to or something interesting to talk about. She's calm and even-tempered as she works rapidly on the client sitting in her chair while simultaneously throwing remarks over her shoulder to the throng of observers standing mesmerized behind her.

"Hello, gorgeous *(her salutation for everyone—no wonder we all flock to her!)*," she addressed me one Thursday morning as I walked into her home/salon in Brooklyn. It was 10:00 A.M., but she was already hard at work on the coiffure of an elderly woman who sat in her chair. "What's doing, Rickey?" she asked. "How's the interviewing coming along?"

"Oh, Georgie!" I sighed in bliss. "I just *love* my work. I keep on meeting the most wonderful people and hear the most amazing stories."

In 1995, I had begun working for an organization that collected audiovisual histories of Holocaust survivors. I went into their homes and interviewed them at length, recording in detail the history of their lives before, during, and after the war. On a personal level, I was particularly fascinated by what happened afterwards—how these survivors coped and refashioned their lives in the aftermath of such horror. It was inspiring for me to witness their ability to re-create in America the lives they had seemingly lost forever in Europe.

Just yesterday, I mused as I watched Georgie's fingers fly, I had interviewed a Hungarian woman named Chana Lebowitz,* who had fashioned a meaningful life for herself despite the great personal losses that she had sustained. She had made a deep impression on me, and I had been very moved by our talk. I had been fascinated by her description of a rather unique labor camp in which she had been incarcerated in 1944—a labor camp called Parshnitz which I had never heard of before.

"It was an all-women's camp," Mrs. Lebowitz had told me. "It was out in the country and consisted of farmland. We had to work the gardens, and whenever we could, we picked cabbages to place in our shirts, to make us seem robust. If we looked frail and thin, we were 'selected.' Those cabbages helped many of us survive."

Her words echoed in my mind as I stood behind Georgie and observed her wizardry. Until yesterday, I had not even been aware that an all-women's labor camp had existed, and I wondered how many other people were aware of it. I was fairly literate in concentration camp history, yet the very notion of this camp was a revelation to me. I had never met anyone from Parshnitz before, and had never encountered its name anywhere else.

As I studied Georgie at her craft, I also thought about my own daughters—teenagers now—and what a different life they had from this woman, who had been their age at the time of her internment. How vulnerable she had been—and to what great lengths she had gone to disguise this very vulnerability. My daughters had radiant, healthy skin, lustrous hair, shining eyes. They didn't need to engage in the pretense that they were healthy or depend on cabbages to avoid certain death.

"So, Rickey," Georgie said, interrupting my reveries. She motioned toward the woman sitting in her chair. "You know . . . Mrs. Schwartz* is *also* a survivor . . . maybe you could interview her right now!"

Georgie was a great champion of my work. And she always liked to encourage people to maximize every opportunity that came their way.

"Oh, would you mind?" I said, turning to the elderly

woman eagerly.

"Well," she hesitated, "I really haven't spoken of it all these years. . . . The pain is so intense still . . . to this day. . . . But I have to face the fact that my generation is dying out, and now there are these Holocaust 'deniers' going around saying it never even happened. . . . I guess it is our duty to speak out, to tell the next generation, before we all disappear. Yes, I will talk to you. . . . What would you like to know?"

I whipped out my pen and pad. "Well, first of all, in which camp or camps were you interned? Auschwitz? Buna? Buchenwald?"

"Oh, no," she shook her head. "I wasn't in a concentration camp at all, thank God. I had the 'good fortune,' if you can call it that, to be in a labor camp. But you probably never heard of it; no one ever has. . . . It was a small, obscure all-women's farm camp. Funny thing . . . what I remember most vividly about my time there is a ploy we girls would use to help keep alive. We would filch cabbages from the gardens, and fill our blouses with them to disguise how thin and emaciated we really were. . . . "

My jaw dropped, my eyes widened, and there was a catch in my throat.

How could this be? I wondered. *I had only heard of such a camp for the first time less than a day ago. It couldn't be the same camp, could it?*

I tried to keep my face composed. "What was the name of the camp—do you remember?" I asked.

"Parshnitz," she said.

"Did you by any chance know a girl who was there by the name of Chana Stern (Mrs. Lebowitz's maiden name)?" I asked casually.

Her face crumpled. "My best friend in the camp," she said. "I lost her after the war. I heard she died."

I laid my hand gently on her shoulder. "Mrs. Schwartz, I don't know how to tell you this . . . but what you heard is simply not true. I interviewed Chana Stern myself . . . just yesterday. She is very much alive, thank God."

Mrs. Stern turned pale and was silent for a few seconds.

"Where does she live today?" she asked, finally summoning up the words after some of the shock had dissipated.

"On Fiftieth Street between Fourteenth and Fifteenth Avenues in Borough Park," I said.

"Rickey," Georgie interjected urgently, "Mrs. Schwartz lives on Fifty-First Street between Fourteenth and Fifteenth Avenues!"

"How long has she been living there?" Mrs. Schwartz asked in disbelief.

"I think about thirty-five years," I answered.

"Unbelievable!" she sighed, tears springing to her eyes. "We've lived around the corner from each other, and never met all these years . . . not even once! . . . Do you have her phone number?" she asked.

"Of course," I answered.

As I said before, going to Georgie's is never an ordinary experience. Somehow it always turns into . . . an event!

*A*s I approached my twenty-third birthday with nothing to show for it but a string of bad dates, each worse than the previous one, I was almost ready to give up on ever finding my soul mate. Then my Aunt Rivky, who lives in Israel, told me that many people go to the Western Wall to pray for their soul mate. Specifically, she told me, praying there for forty days in a row was a blessing and had brought many couples to the marriage canopy.

I must admit that I was skeptical, but I knew that praying at the Western Wall could certainly do no harm. And if my own personal prayer was not answered, perhaps it would help someone else in Israel. So I decided to go ahead and, as the advertising slogan says, "Just do it!" With the help of Aunt Rivky, I made arrangements to rent a room in the neighborhood of Jerusalem called the German Colony, which is within walking distance of the Wall. I took exactly forty days off from work (I had a very understanding boss) and flew from New York to the holy city with no small amount of trepidation.

I had been to Israel many times before, but never on my own. My aunt had arranged for me to rent one room in the apartment of an American-born woman. Sara was in her late thirties, still single, and very bitter. She seemed to hate me from the minute we met. The reasons weren't hard to fathom. With every movement, every gesture, every shrug, her attitude implied: *Where do you get the nerve to worry about being single? What's the emergency? You're only twenty-three years old. I, on the other hand, am almost forty. My biological clock is ticking. Yours is just fine. I don't know if I'll ever get married and have children. You still have prospects. You have some chutzpah to think it's you who's in crisis!*

Far from home, I was hurt to encounter such overt hostility—but I tried to understand her perspective. If *I* was suffering, how much greater must be *her* pain and torment? I ached for her. I was far younger than she, and my possibilities were less bleak. So I tried to overcome her animosity by explaining the purpose of my trip. As I launched into my recital, she could not help but be intrigued. Although she lived in Israel herself, she had never heard about the forty-day prayer ritual. So when I urged her to join me, she set aside her antagonism and agreed to accompany me.

Every day, for forty consecutive days, Sara and I went faithfully to the Western Wall for morning services and to recite a special prayer for a soul mate. From there, Sara would go off to work, while I would head for studies at Neve Yerushalayim Teachers Seminary, where I was temporarily enrolled. We repeated this scenario regularly every single day without fail. It wasn't easy! Even though I had come to Israel for this purpose and this purpose only, there were mornings when I almost didn't make it in time for morning prayers. There were mishaps; obstacles; delays that seemed to conspire against me and stymie efforts constantly. Yet I was determined. Despite the hardships that confronted me, I managed to complete a full sequence of forty days in a row. Then it was time to go home.

I hopped a plane that took me back to New York, back to my job, and back to my parents' home, where I waited for someone special to appear. Obligingly, he arrived on schedule—just a few short months after my return from Israel—and joyfully we set our wedding date for the night of *Tu B'Av*—an auspicious time in the Jewish calendar. As I mailed out my wedding invitations, I thought of my old roommate Sara, and impulsively decided to send her one, too. I did not really expect her to travel so far, but I wanted to notify her of my good news. In response, I received a note from her saying: "Thank you for inviting me to your wedding, but I'm sorry I won't be able to attend. You see, I will be getting married on the exact same night myself. *Mazel Tov!*"

Sure enough, inside the envelope was an invitation to *her* wedding scheduled for . . . *Tu B'Av.*

—*Ayala Cohen*

*I*n most countries around the world, it's unsafe to hitch a ride with a stranger, but not in Israel, which still retains the *haimish* (homey) warmth of a large, squabbling family. Despite the great religious and political divide that pits brother against brother in the tiny Jewish state, it's not uncommon to see skullcapped, long-bearded men stop on the road for bareheaded jeans-clad strangers, and vice versa. The camaraderie in the cars is easygoing, and a spirit of adventure prevails. Despite the perils—which some might consider especially pronounced in a country with so much unrest—"tramping" (hitchhiking) remains a popular mode of travel for the carless.

Yitzchok Tessler works in the ancient, mystical city of Tzefat (also called Sfad), but lives in the barely inhabited village of Miron. Miron is famous for being home to the burial site of one of the greatest Jewish sages of all time, Rabbi Shimon Bar Yochai. Pilgrims from all over the world wend their way to the *kever* (grave site) for prayers, and during the day buses and automobiles discharge passengers at a regular clip. Morning, afternoon, and evening, the area is overrun by a constant, endless stream of petitioners, and sounds of weeping, wailing, and excited chatter fill the air. By nightfall, however, most of the pilgrims are gone, and an eerie silence descends.

"Not too many people travel to Miron at night," says Mr. Tessler. He works as the manager of the Kol Tuv Restaurant, which closes late. "That is why I am always astonished and overcome with gratitude to Hashem (God) that somehow I always manage to get a tramp home from Tzefat, despite the unusual hour. I never cease to be amazed by my good fortune, and always ask my benefactor why he is going to Miron at such a strange time. Working in Tzefat as I do, few things surprise me anymore, but sometimes the answers sound more like ancient Hasidic tales than like contemporary accounts, and fill my soul with awe and wonder. This was my exact experience on the night of May 30, 2000, one week after the Jewish festival of *Lag B'Omer*, when thousands of Jews had gathered at Rabbi Shimon Bar Yochai's grave site in Miron to commemorate the anniversary of his death.

"The massive crowds that had flocked to Miron for the festival had long dispersed, and once again I was standing on the lonely road leading out of Tzefat, wondering pensively if I would be able to find a tramp home. When an unfamiliar car rolled to a stop in front of me, I was surprised to note the identity of the driver.

"Dr. Horwitz* is a famous professor who teaches at the University of Tzefat. He is not an observant Jew, and certainly not the type to make a pilgrimage to Miron late at night. When he told me that Rabbi Shimon Bar Yochai's grave site was indeed his destination, I could not help but raise my eyebrows in surprise.

"'I hope you don't mind my asking,' I said as I gratefully slid into the front seat next to him, 'but what are you doing going to Miron at this hour?'

"He hesitated for a fraction of a second. 'Well,' he said, 'I certainly don't mind telling you if you promise not to laugh. . . .'

"'Many years ago,' he began, 'I adopted an adorable six-week-old puppy that I named Benny. Since I am a bachelor and live alone, I became very attached to my pet.

'Benny was easily trainable and I really didn't even have to walk him if I didn't want to. He learned to scratch at the front door with his paws and bark meaningfully, and that signaled me that he wanted to go out. I would open the door, he'd scamper out, and he'd return like clockwork after about a half-hour absence. In Tzefat, where there are few automobiles compared with other cities and only benign tourists, I never worried about Benny's whereabouts. I knew he would always come home.

'But when Benny turned one year old, something strange began to happen. I never really timed his outings, but it suddenly dawned on me one night that he was taking an unusually long time to return home. It seemed as if certainly more than a half-hour had elapsed. Maybe it was even an hour since he had left? "Where have you been?" I scolded him affectionately when he finally returned, happily wagging his tail. I wondered idly what canine adventures he had pursued that had resulted in both his length absence and the unusual exuberance he radiated. On second thought, it seemed to me that Benny had actually been gone even longer than one hour; at least an hour and a half had passed, I realized.

'Things settled back into their usual routine, and more pressing matters than my dog's adventures consumed my thoughts. But exactly one week later, Benny disappeared again. And as on the previous occasion, he didn't return for almost two hours. I was mildly curious, but not alarmed. *Maybe he's found himself a lady friend,* I thought.

'By the third week, my curiosity was genuinely piqued, because I had suddenly realized that there was a definite pattern underlying Benny's mysterious outings. *Hey,* I muttered to myself one night, as consciousness finally dawned. *He only disappears on Friday nights!*

'And then another piece of the puzzle fell into place as it struck me . . . *and always around sunset!*

'By the fourth week, I could no longer contain my curiosity. *I have to know where Benny's going once and for all,* I vowed fiercely. *I can't take it anymore.*

'Friday evening, when the hush that had descended over Tzefat announced the advent of the Sabbath, Benny scratched on the front door with his paws and barked meaningfully. I let him out and waited a second or two; then I followed in hot pursuit. From a discreet distance,

I shadowed my dog stealthily. I was seriously intent on my mission, but inside part of me had to laugh. What a scene! A middle-aged university professor with a Ph.D., furtively stalking his very own dog! But I just had to know where he went every Friday night . . . the mystery was driving me to distraction!

'When I finally discovered Benny's destination, the mystery only deepened, however. For his destination was none other than a *beit haknesset* (synagogue) where Sabbath evening prayers were being loudly chanted by a roomful of congregants!

'I watched Benny slip into the synagogue, slink into a corridor adjoining the main sanctuary, and lie down next to the connecting door, from whence a crack of light appeared and the sound of the worshipers' prayers could clearly be heard. Benny lay quietly—almost reverentially—during the entire length of the prayer service, and only when the last prayer was uttered did he get up and leave for home. Had I not observed the entire scene with my own two eyes, I never would have believed it.

'*Must be an aberration,* I thought. *Surely this is not where he disappears to every single Friday night. Why would Benny go to shul?*

'So, the following Friday night, I turned sleuth again. As was now becoming the norm, Benny left home at about sunset, and once more I followed surreptitiously from behind. This time, I was relieved to see him trot in a completely different direction from the previous week. I wasn't entirely thrilled to think he attended synagogue every Friday night. I myself am a nonbeliever. What would I do with a spiritual dog?

'But it was, eventually, to a synagogue after all that he hastened; it was just a different one from the previous week. This time, Benny didn't enter the building, but lay outside instead, beneath an open window, and cocked his ears attentively to the prayers being chanted by the worshipers inside. As on the previous Friday, Benny didn't move from his position below the window until the final prayer had been completed and the congregants began to move towards the door.

'I followed Benny a few more times after that, and the scenario basically repeated itself with just a few variations. Benny didn't seem loyal to any one particular synagogue—he moved around a lot. Sometimes he attended Sephardic (Middle Eastern) services, and other times he worshiped at Ashkenazic (European) shuls. He seemed to like them all.

'Well, after a few weeks of shadowing Benny, I got tired and gave up the chase. I figured he was safe in synagogue, and if he wanted to be observant, it was his business, not mine. Thus, his Friday night visits to synagogues throughout Tzefat continued regularly for many years.'

"Here the professor abruptly broke off his story and stared into the inky darkness of the road ahead.

"So why are you going to Miron now?" Yitchok Tessler asked the professor, confused by his tale. "I don't understand. What is the connection between your dog Benny and your own visit to Miron tonight?"

"Oh," said the professor thoughtfully, rubbing his forehead in distraction. "Well, here's what happened. Last week, on the eve of the Jewish festival of *Lag B'Omer*, Benny disappeared again. But this time he didn't come back, and I'm worried sick. He's been missing for more than seven days. I've hunted for him all over Tzefat, and there's no trace of him anywhere.

"Finally, one of my neighbors advised me to search for him in Miron. 'Tens of thousands of Jews from all over the world travel to Miron to participate in the *hilula* (commemoration) of Rabbi Shimon Bar Yochai on *Lag B'Omer*,' she said. 'Who knows? A dog who attends prayer services on the Sabbath might be the kind of dog who participates in *Lag B'Omer* festivities in Miron. Maybe that's where you should look.'

"So I took her advice and now I'm on my way to Miron to look for my holy dog!"

$\mathcal{T}$*alk* about instant gratification and immediate results!

Rachel Fox* had just cried her eyes out inside the women's section of Amuka, the legendary grave site in Israel of Rabbi Yonatan Ben Uziel, the fabled matchmaker for singles in trouble. Rachel was thirty-five and never married.

She had tried everything—earthly matchmakers, singles parties, personal ads—but nothing had worked. When all else fails, her friends had advised, a trip to Amuka is the last resort.

Stories of the amazing successes brought about by Amuka's "magic" abounded. Everyone had a tale to tell of a single person thwarted in his or her futile quest to find a mate, who finally made the long trip to Amuka at the behest of frantic friends and family (usually mothers!) and miraculously found a mate only a week or a month later. Rachel Fox's friends finally prevailed on her, and off to Amuka she went.

Inside the women's section, Rachel wept and wailed, adding her melodious alto to the female chorus keening near her. Several buses from a women's seminary had discharged dozens of students as she entered the tomb site, and the crush made her labor for air.

As she extricated herself from the densely packed crowd and exited, Rachel found that she was still in a crowd, for there were multitudes outside as well. It was a busy summer day, the height of tourist season, and it was *Tu B'Av* (the fifteenth of *Av*) to boot. During the era of the second temple, *Tu B'Av* was the traditional day when single women dressed in their finest flowing white gowns and danced in circles while eligible men observed from the sidelines, looking for a woman who struck a chord in their heart. While this specific tradition was no longer practiced, *Tu B'Av* was still considered a particularly felicitous time to hunt for a mate. The day was celebrated as a harbinger of blessings . . . and miracles.

Crowds thronged the plaza near the tombstone, pushing and shoving cheerfully. Trying to fight the human tide that swept her along involuntarily, Rachel was mortified to discover that she had accidentally ground one of her spiked heels into a young man's big toe.

He yelped.

She stammered apologies.

He smiled good-naturedly.

She blushed. He asked her whether she were just going into Amuka, or leaving.

She was on her way out, she explained.

"Me, too," he said. "First time I've been here. But I'm thirty-eight and my parents are frantic. . . . So . . . do you think it works?" he twinkled.

It didn't take long for the two to become immersed in deep conversation. At nightfall, they were still standing in the parking area talking, oblivious to their surroundings, heedless of the fact that theirs were the only two cars left in the lot. (They also failed to notice the wild bulls that wander near Amuka and make crowds scatter. The bulls—possibly realizing that something momentous was taking place—gave the couple a wide berth.) By midnight, both realized that a return trip to Amuka would probably be unnecessary. At least not a return trip armed with petitions or appeals. Perhaps only thanks for answered prayers would bring them back again.

The legend of Amuka goes on.

*L*eah Lange, a resident of Oak Park, Michigan, attended a lecture on November 5, 2000, by Yitta Halberstam, coauthor of this book and other titles in the *Small Miracles* series. After the lecture, she bought the latest book *Small Miracles for Women* and took it home—never dreaming that it would change her life.

In the book, she read a story that she found particularly riveting. When she got to the end, she stared in shock at the byline. The story was written by Molly Gordy—her long-lost best friend from childhood, a woman whom she had been unsuccessfully trying to track down for more than thirty years! Could it be the very same woman she had sought for so long?

Fortunately, she and Yitta had exchanged e-mail addresses after the author's talk. Excitedly, Mrs. Lange e-mailed her and asked if she knew where to contact Molly Gordy. She did. She e-mailed back Molly's New York phone number and asked to be kept apprised of the unfolding drama.

A few hours later, Lange e-mailed Yitta again, this time in jubilation and triumph. She had found her long-lost friend! She told Yitta: "Wonder of wonders, miracle of miracles—I have found my dearest childhood friend. Our mothers were pregnant together, we painted our tennis shoes blue together and turned our high school gym class upside down! We had a wonderful chat about the last thirty years."

The lives of the two friends had gone in totally different directions, Leah told Yitta. Both had grown up together in Milwaukee, Wisconsin, but after graduation they had gone their separate ways. "Molly left for Europe and then moved to New York to make it big as an award-winning journalist, and I went to Israel and became a *ba'alat teshuvah* (returnee to Judaism). Now Molly teaches journalism at Columbia University and I am Oak Park's *'mikveh* lady' (in charge of the community ritual baths)."

Leah reported that Molly had been "totally freaked out" when she called, and they made plans to meet soon.

Leah's e-mail to Yitta concluded: "Thank you for being the agent in yet another 'small miracle.'"

Molly Gordy and Yitta met over the phone through another serendipitous event. Gordy, then working at the *New York Daily News* as an investigative journalist, had fished out a copy of the first *Small Miracles* book from a galley bin in the book review editor's office, and found herself enthralled by the amazing true-life stories. Undergoing a personal crisis at the time, she asked God to please send her a sign that all would be well. At that moment, an unexpected bouquet of flowers was delivered to her desk. Overwhelmed by the coincidence, Molly Gordy picked up the phone and called Yitta to tell her "I believe in small miracles!" A friendship of sorts was formed over the phone, and Yitta enlisted Molly to write a story for *Small Miracles for Women*. After a thunderstruck Leah Lange read this same story one Sabbath afternoon in Michigan, the wheels for the reunion between the two friends were set into motion.

Jubilant at having been the instrument for such a wonderful reunion, Yitta muses thoughtfully: "Interestingly, this particular volume — *Small Miracles for Women* — contains an inordinate number of stories revolving around miraculous reunions of long-lost friends, lovers, and relatives. Now we can say with pride: *Small Miracles* not only recounts reunion stories, it *creates* them!"

Even more Small Miracles

Trade paperback, $9.95,
ISBN: 1-55850-646-2

Trade paperback, $9.95,
ISBN: 1-58062-047-7

Trade paperback, $9.95,
ISBN: 1-58062-180-5

Trade paperback, $9.95,
ISBN: 1-58062-370-0

Four collections of true stories of remarkable coincidences that have changed the lives of ordinary people. These stories, both heartwarming and awe-inspiring, convey that coincidences are more than just random happenings—in fact, they are nothing less than divine messages.

"Judith Leventhal and Yitta Halberstam amaze and inspire with their incredible-but-true story collections . . . "
—*People Magazine*

Available Wherever Books Are Sold

**For more information, or to order, call 800-872-5627
or visit www.adamsmedia.com**

Adams Media Corporation, 57 Littlefield Street, Avon, MA 02322.